RECORDED VERSIONS
GUITAR

**AUTHENTIC TRANSCRIPTIONS
WITH NOTES AND TABLATURE**

W9-BSU-764

GUITAR HERO III
LEGENDS of ROCK
SONGBOOK

Artwork © Activision

ISBN 978-1-4234-4020-8

HAL•LEONARD®
CORPORATION

7777 W. BLUEMOUND RD. P.O. BOX 13819 MILWAUKEE, WI 53213

Visit Hal Leonard Online at
www.halleonard.com

Anarchy in the U.K.

Words and Music by John Lydon, Paul Cook, Stephen Jones and Glen Matlock

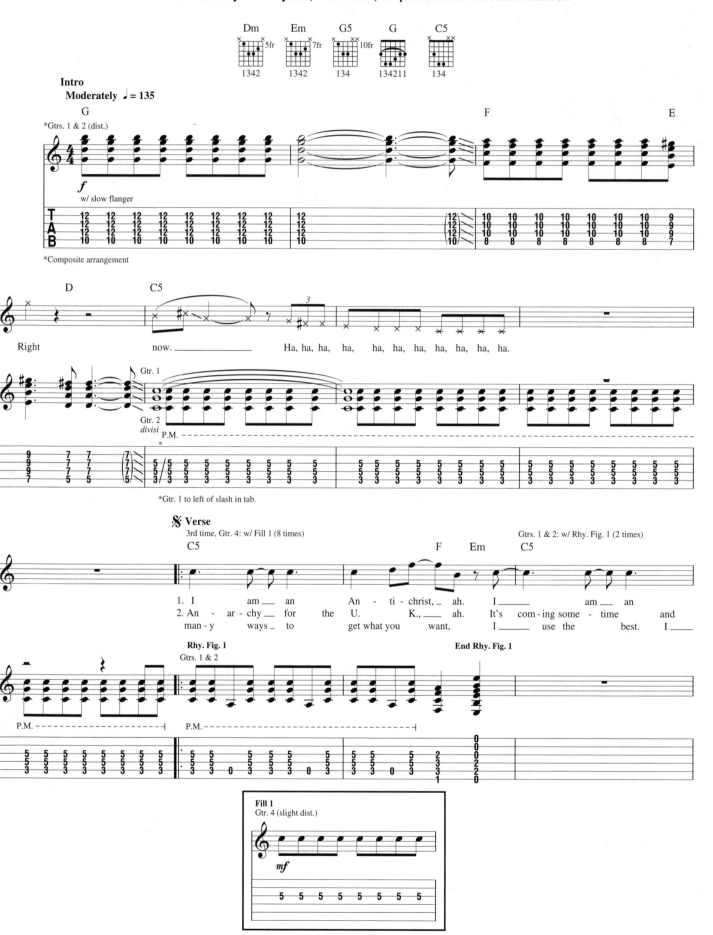

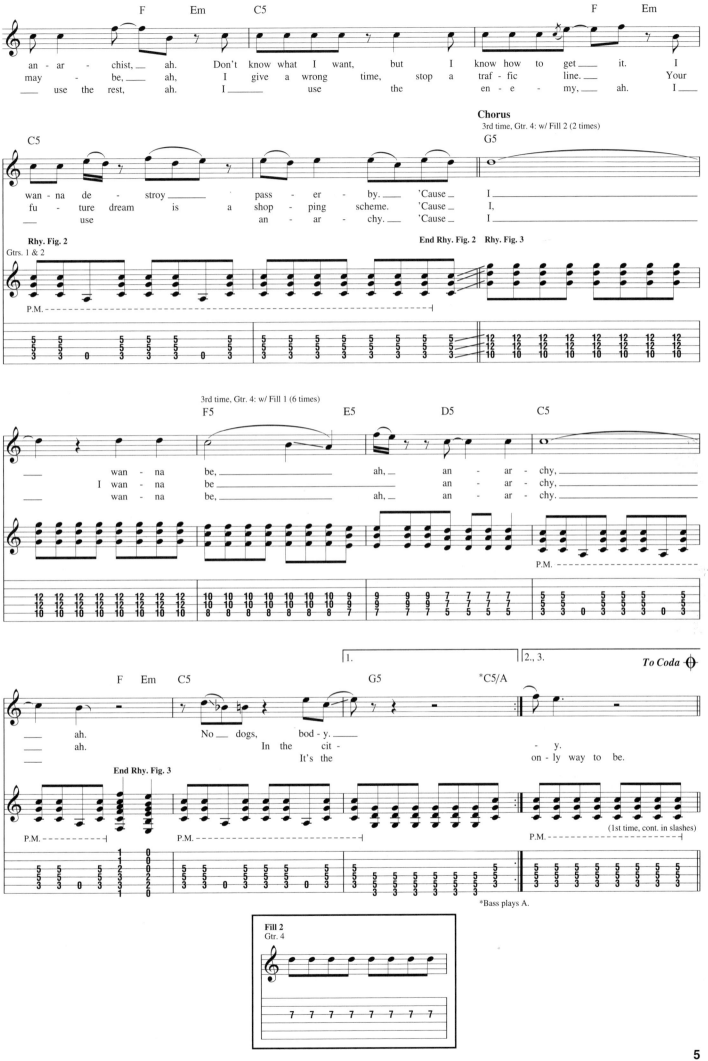

Guitar Solo

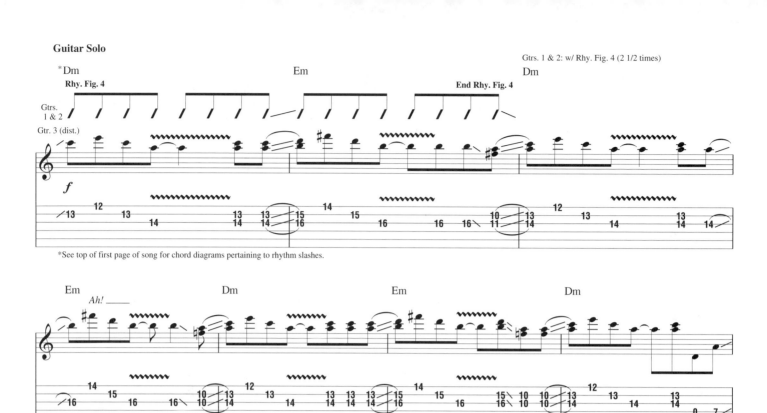

*See top of first page of song for chord diagrams pertaining to rhythm slashes.

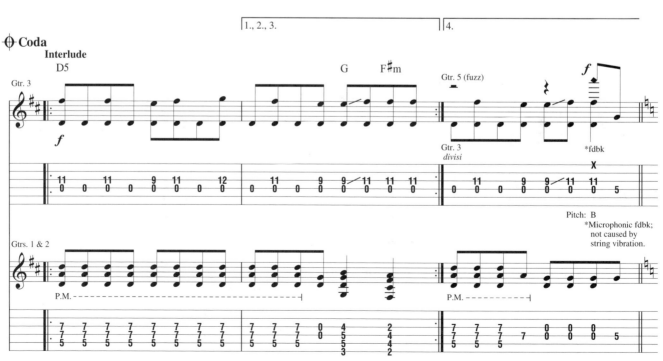

6

Verse

Gtrs. 1 & 2: w/ Rhy. Fig. 1 (3 times)
Gtr. 3 tacet

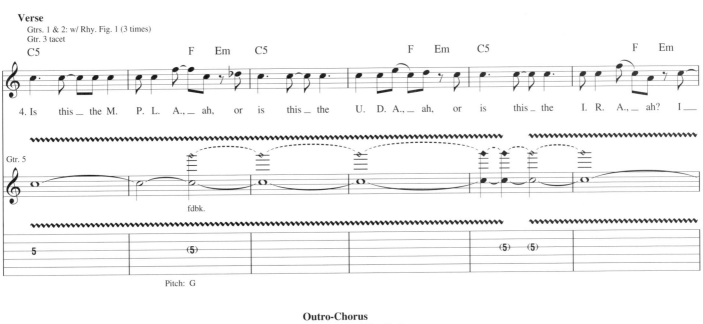

4. Is this __ the M. P. L. A., __ ah, or is this __ the U. D. A., __ ah, or is this __ the I. R. A., __ ah? I __

Pitch: G

Outro-Chorus

Gtrs. 1 & 2: w/ Rhy. Fig. 2

Gtrs. 1 & 2: w/ Rhy. Fig. 3

__ thought __ it was the U. K. __ or just __ an - oth - er __ coun -

Pitch: C

Gtrs. 1 & 2: w/ Rhy. Fig. 2

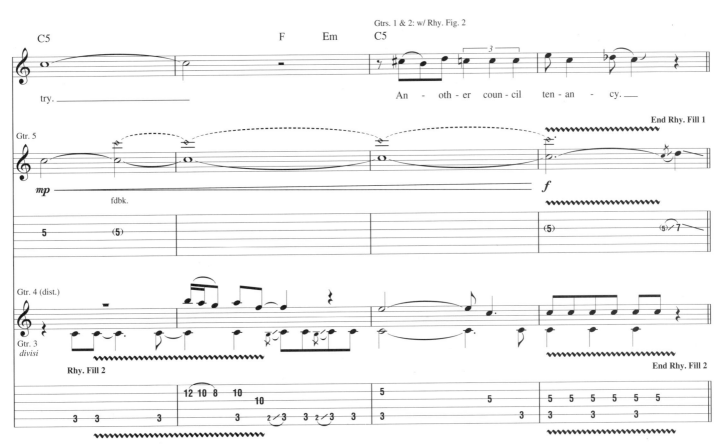

try. __ An - oth - er coun - cil ten - an - cy. __

Pitch: B

Barracuda

Words and Music by Nancy Wilson, Ann Wilson, Michael Derosier and Roger Fisher

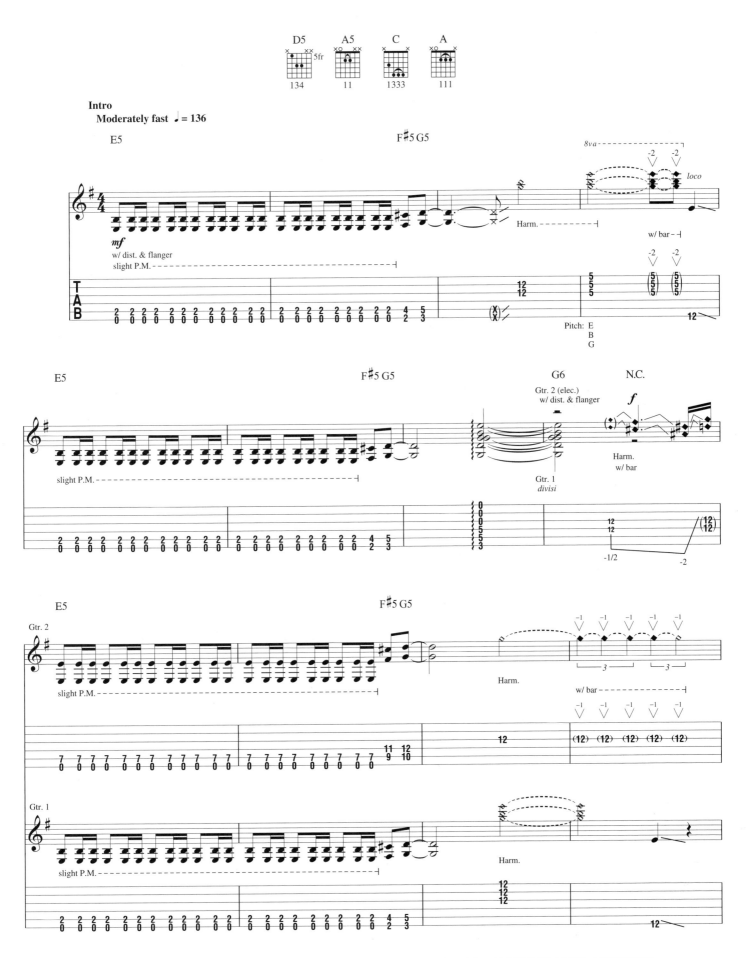

*See top of first page of song for chord diagrams
pertaining to rhythm slashes.

12

Coda 2

Interlude

Gtrs. 1 & 2: w/ Rhy. Figs. 1 & 1A

E5

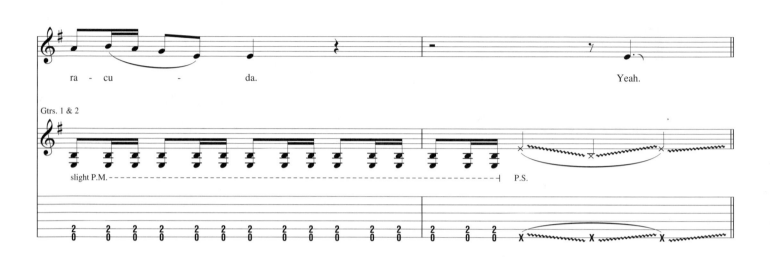

Oh, _____ bar - ra, bar -

ra - cu - da. Yeah.

Gtrs. 1 & 2

slight P.M. - P.S.

Outro

Em7

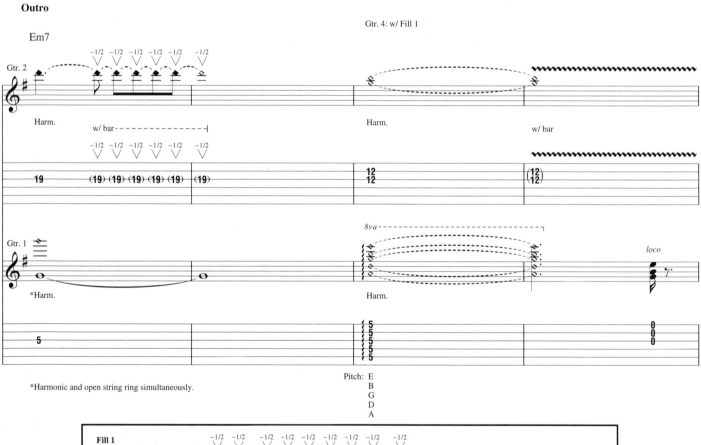

Gtr. 4: w/ Fill 1

Gtr. 2

Harm.   Harm.   w/ bar

w/ bar - - - - - - - - - - - - - -

Gtr. 1

*Harm.   Harm.

8va -

loco

*Harmonic and open string ring simultaneously.

Pitch: E
B
G
D
A

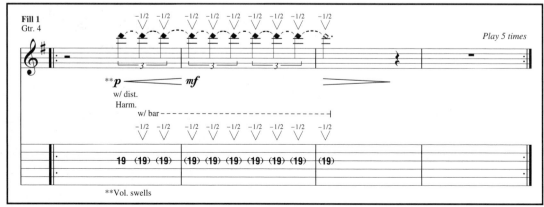

Fill 1
Gtr. 4

Play 5 times

p ——— mf
w/ dist.
Harm.
w/ bar - - - - - - - - - - - - - - - - - -

**Vol. swells

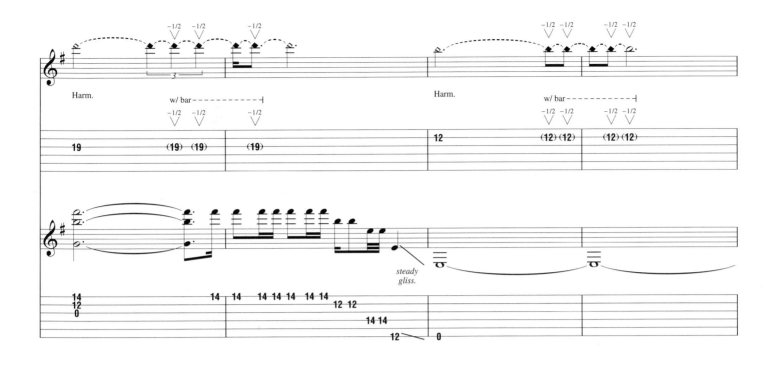

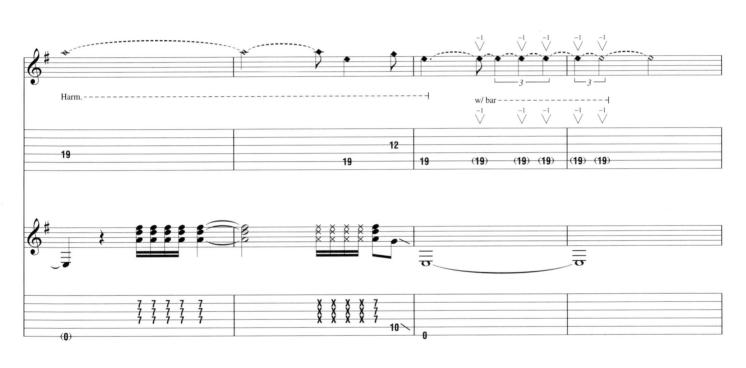

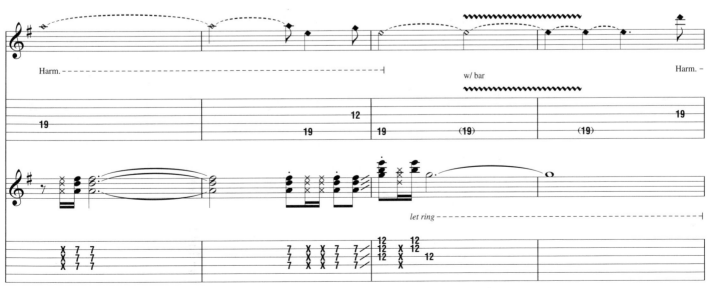

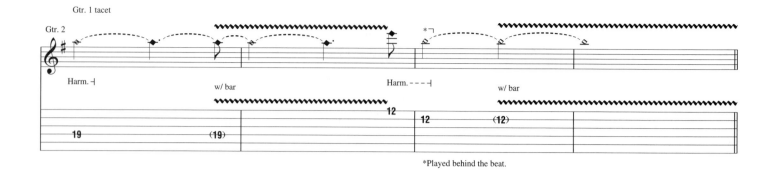

*Played behind the beat.

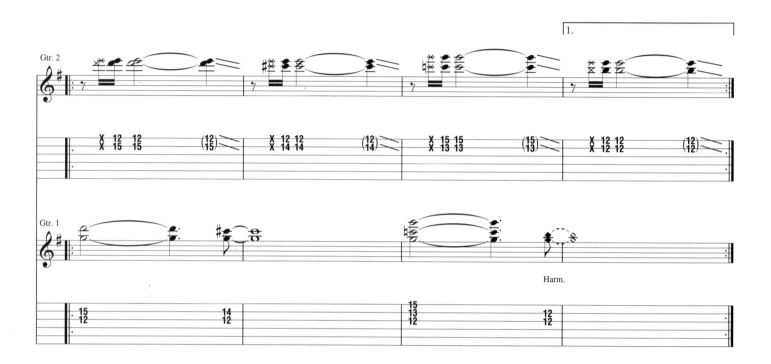

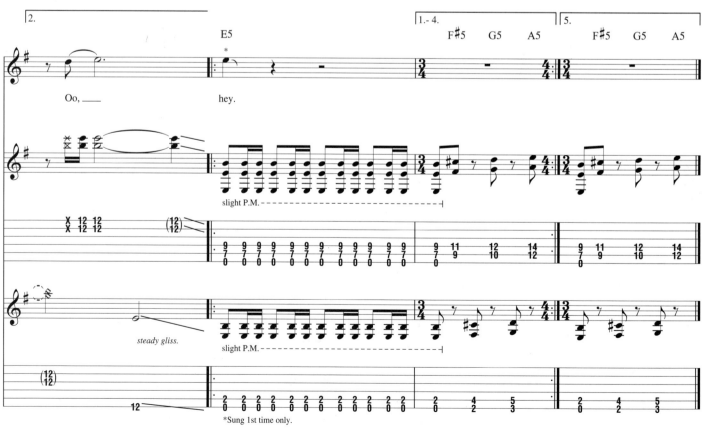

Before I Forget

Words and Music by M. Shawn Crahan, Chris Fehn, Paul Gray, Nathan Jordison,
Corey Taylor, Mic Thompson and Sid Wilson

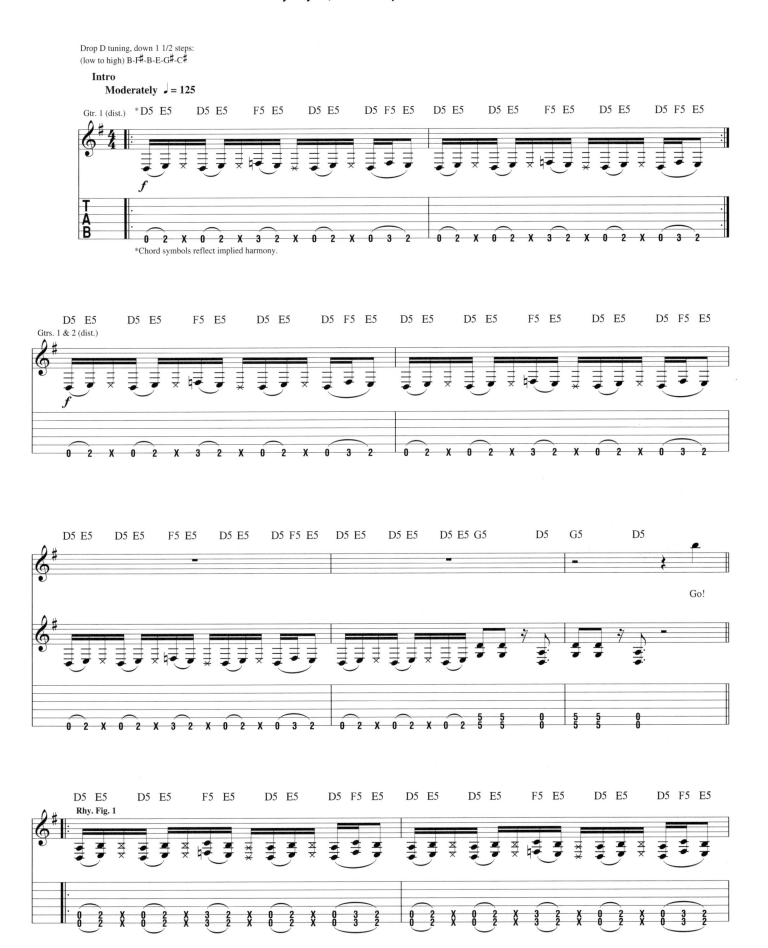

yet I'm the one who's ob - scene. ___ Catch me up ___ on all your sor - did lit - tle in - sur - rec - tions.

I've got no time to lose. ___ I'm just caught up in all the cat - tle.

Pre-Chorus

Spoken: Fray the strings, ___ throw the shapes, ___ hold your breath, ___ lis -ten!

§ Chorus

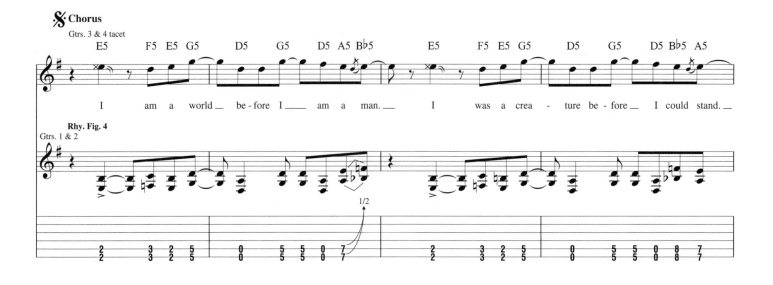

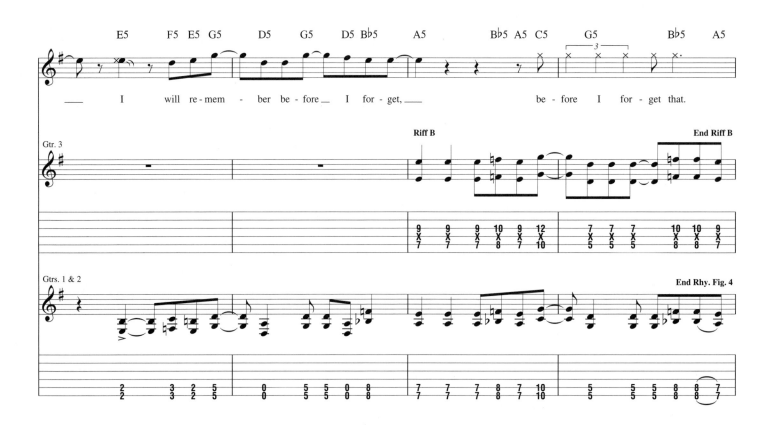

To Coda 1 ⊕

To Coda 2 ⊕

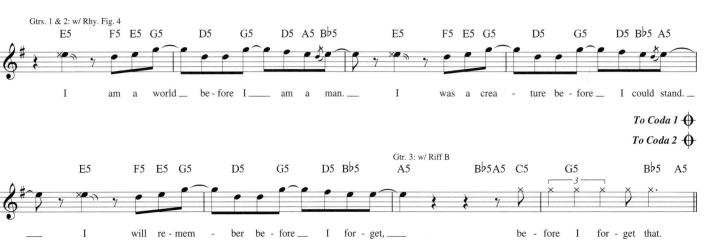

Interlude

Gtrs. 1 & 2: w/ Rhy. Fig. 1

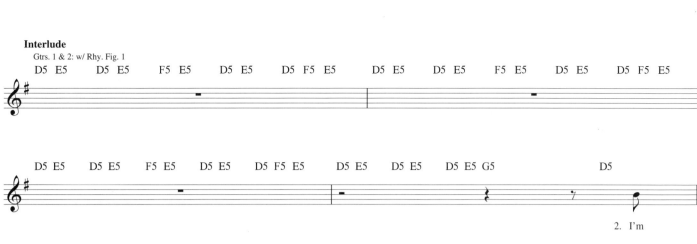

D5 E5   D5 E5   F5 E5   D5 E5   D5 F5 E5   D5 E5   D5 E5   F5 E5   D5 E5   D5 F5 E5

D5 E5   D5 E5   F5 E5   D5 E5   D5 F5 E5   D5 E5   D5 E5   D5 E5 G5   D5

2. I'm

Verse

Gtrs. 1 & 2: w/ Rhy. Fig. 2 (2 times)

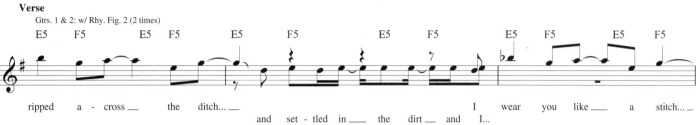

E5   F5   E5   F5   E5   F5   E5   F5   E5   F5   E5   F5

ripped a - cross ___ the ditch... ___ and set - tled in ___ the dirt ___ and I... I wear you like ___ a stitch... ___

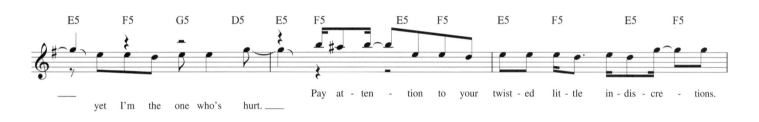

E5   F5   G5   D5   E5   F5   E5   F5   E5   F5   E5   F5

___ yet I'm the one who's hurt. ___ Pay at - ten - tion to your twist - ed lit - tle in - dis - cre - tions.

E5   F5   E5   F5   E5   F5   G5   D5

I've got no right to win. I'm just caught up in all the bat - tles.

D.S. al Coda 1

Pre-Chorus

Gtrs. 1, 2 & 3: w/ Rhy. Figs. 3, 3A & 3B
Gtr. 4: w/ Riff A

E5   F5 E5   F5 E5   F5 E5   F5

Spoken: Locked in clutch, ___ pushed in place, ___ hold your breath, ___ lis - ten!

⊕ Coda 1

Interlude
Half-time feel

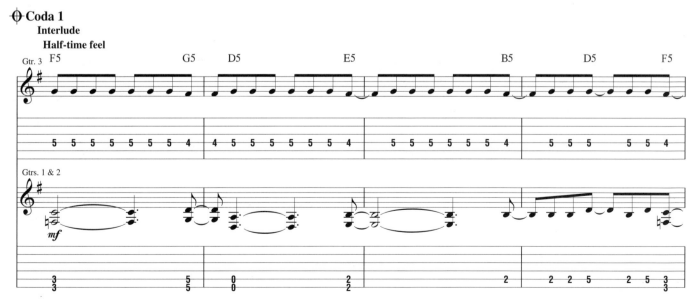

Gtr. 3   F5   G5   D5   E5   B5   D5   F5

Gtrs. 1 & 2

23

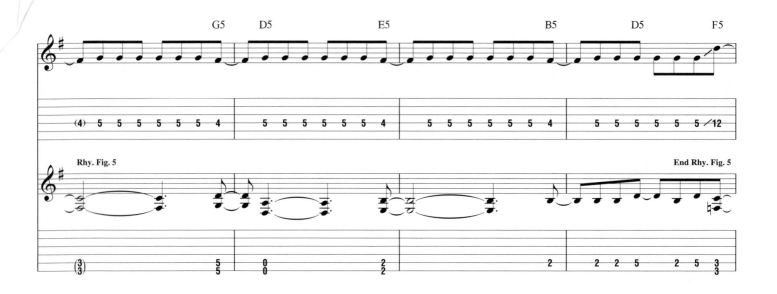

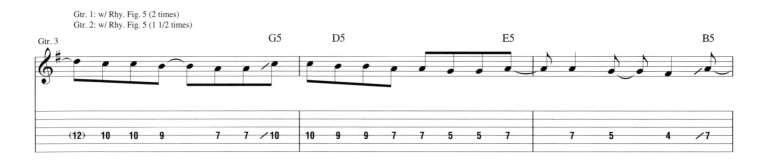

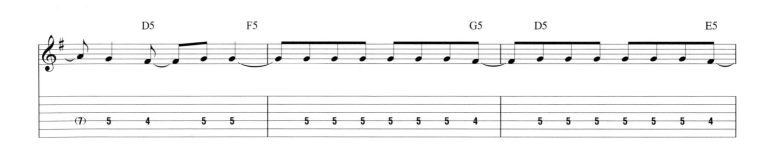

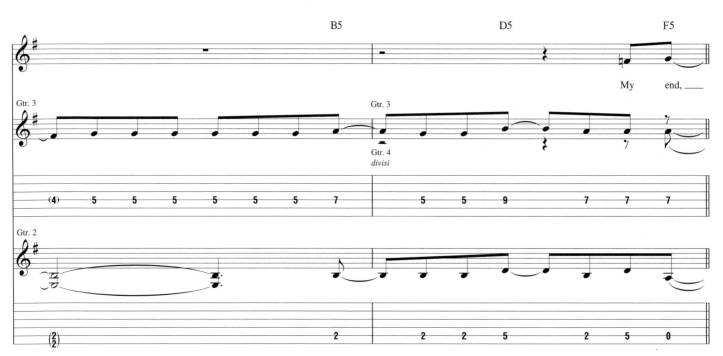

Bridge

Gtr. 3 tacet

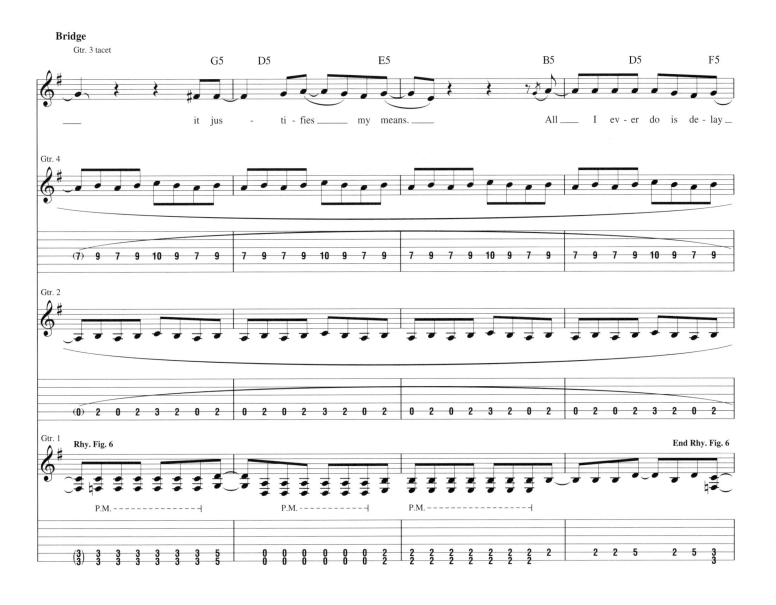

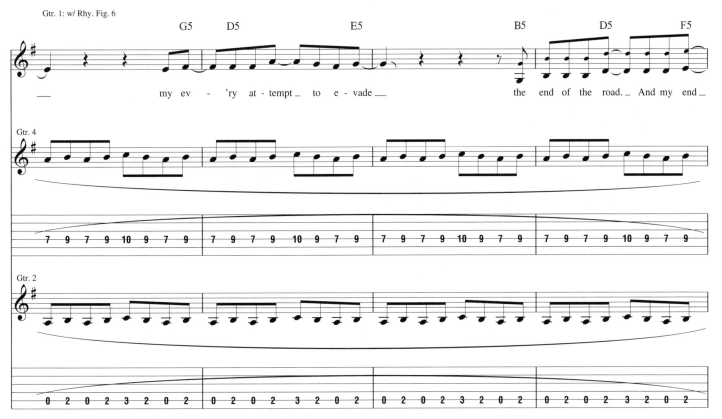

it jus - ti - fies my means. All I ev - er do is de - lay

D.S. al Coda 2
End half-time feel

my ev - 'ry at - tempt to e - vade the end of the road!

 **Coda 2**

Chorus

Gtrs. 1 & 2: w/ Rhy. Fig. 4

I am a world __ be-fore I __ am a man. __ I was a crea - ture be-fore __ I could stand. __

__ I will re - mem - ber be - fore __ I for - get, ___ be - fore I for - get that! __

Outro

Gtrs. 1 & 2

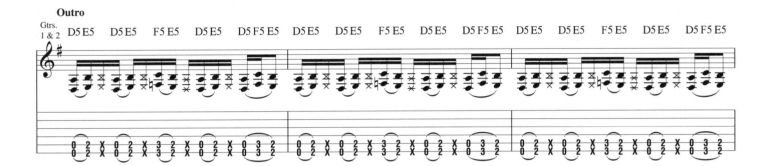

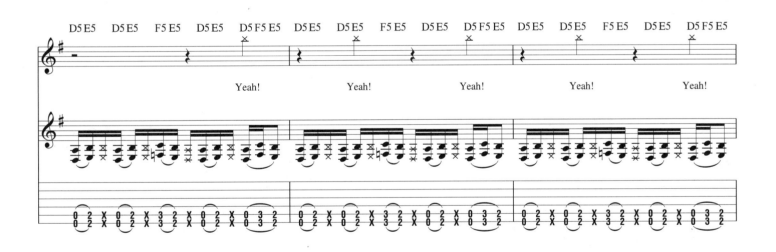

Yeah! Yeah! Yeah! Yeah! Yeah!

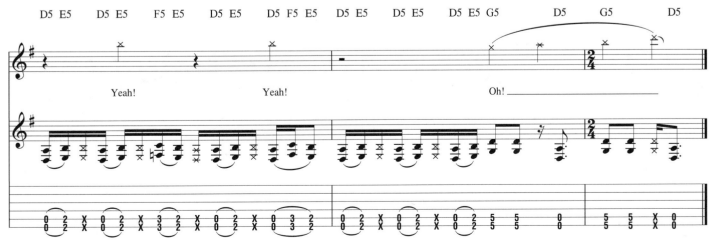

Yeah! Yeah! Oh! __

Black Magic Woman

Words and Music by Peter Green

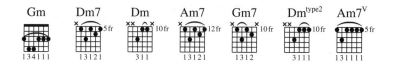

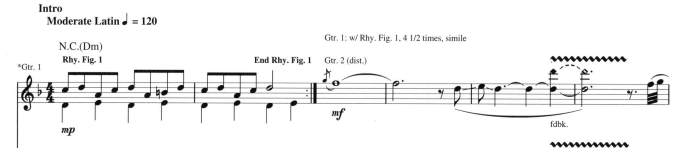

Intro
Moderate Latin ♩ = 120

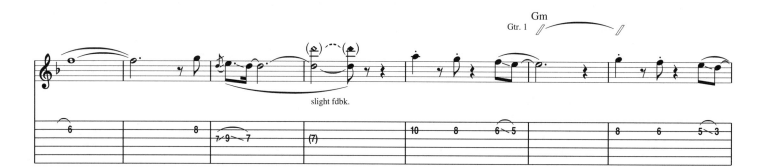

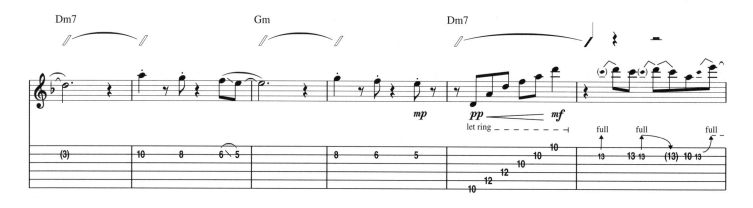

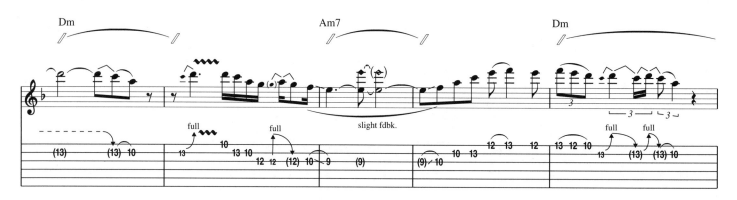

28

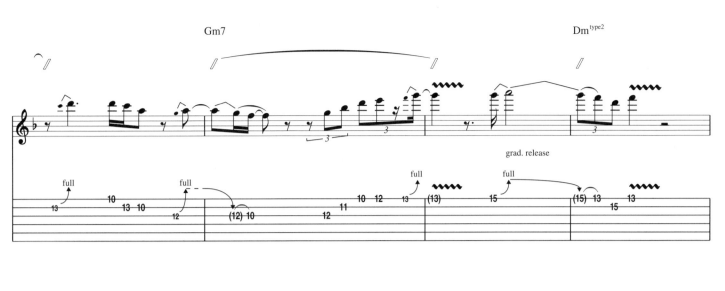

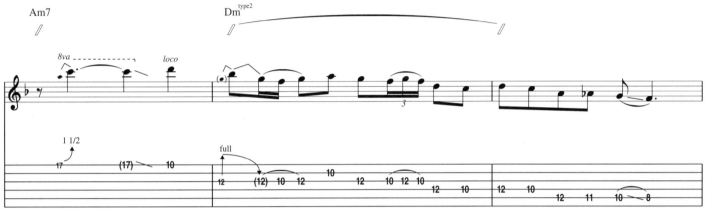

Verse

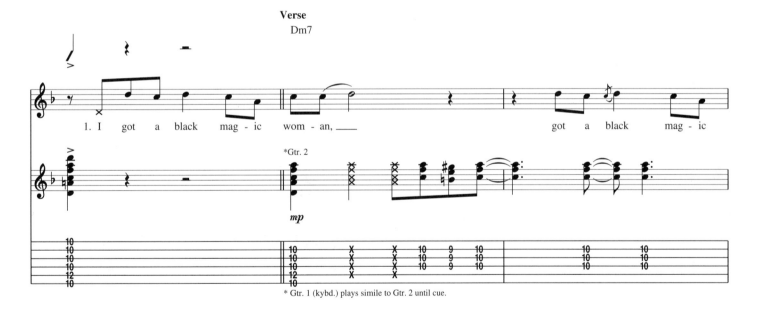

* Gtr. 1 (kybd.) plays simile to Gtr. 2 until cue.

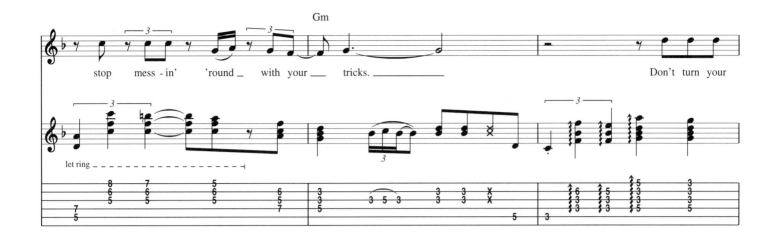

stop mess-in' 'round __ with your __ tricks. _____ Don't turn your

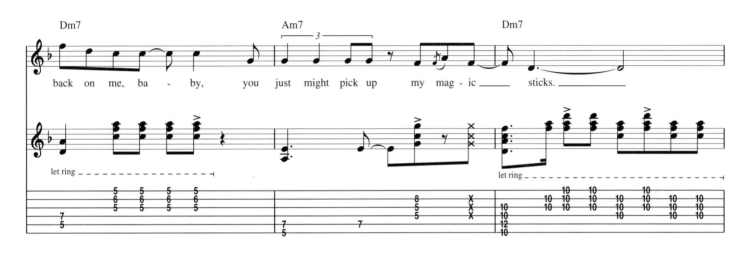

back on me, ba — by, you just might pick up my mag-ic _____ sticks. _____

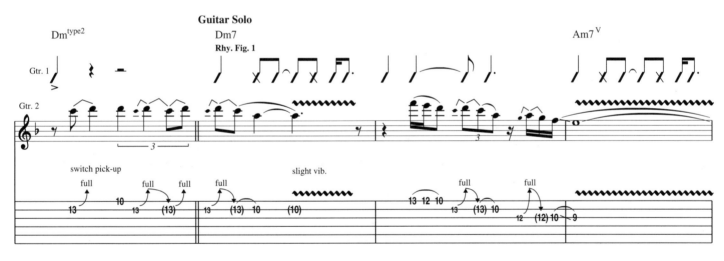

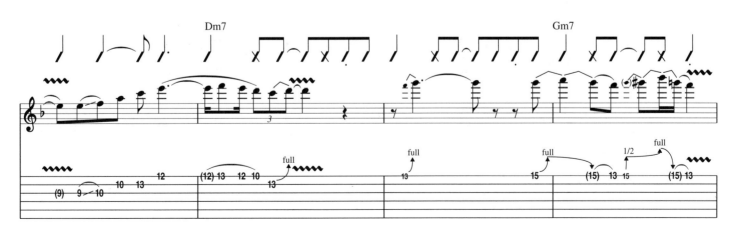

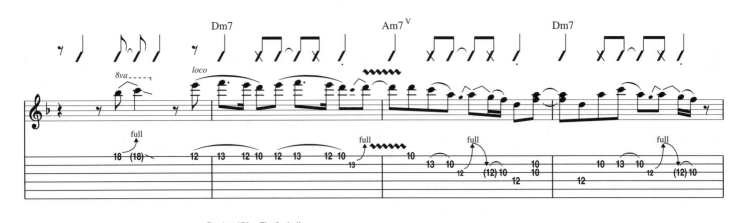

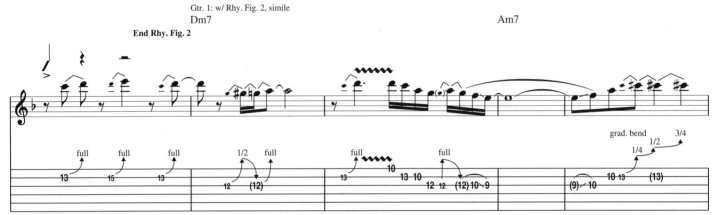

Gtr. 1: w/ Rhy. Fig. 2, simile

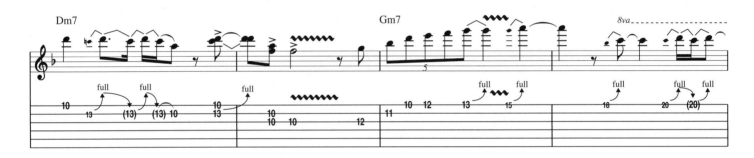

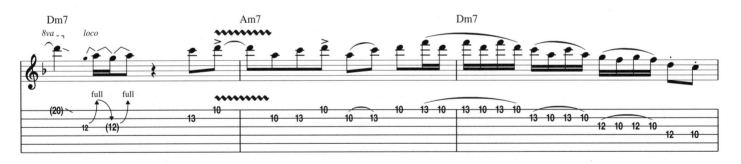

Verse

Gtr. 1: w/ Rhy. Fig. 2, 1st 11 meas., simile

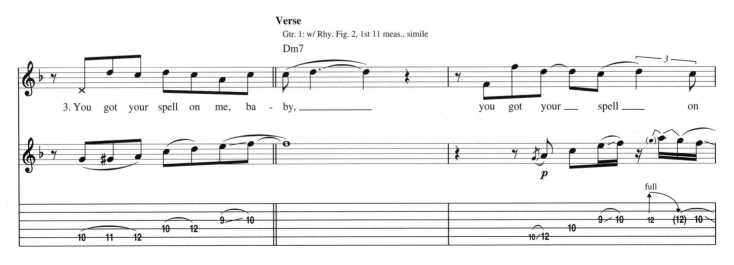

3. You got your spell on me, ba - by, _____ you got your ___ spell ___ on

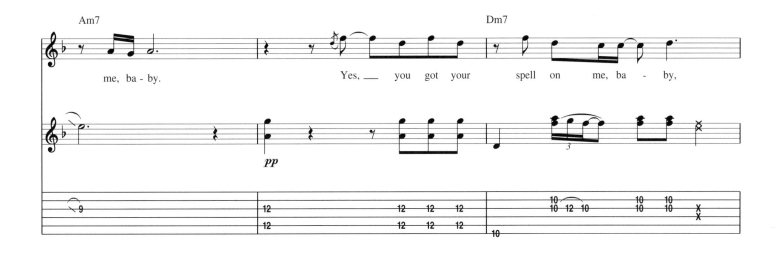

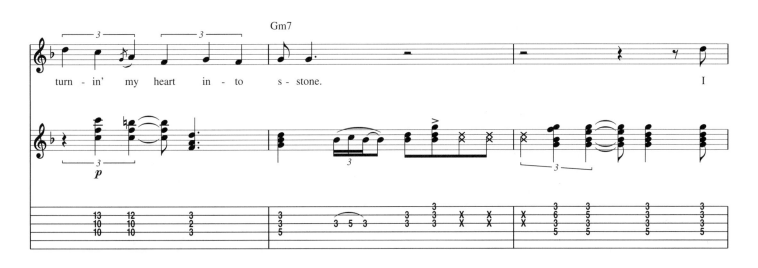

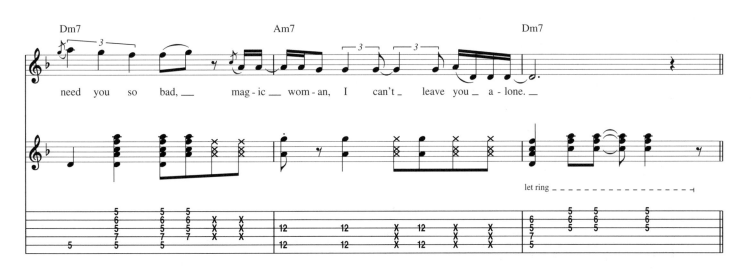

Outro

Gtr. 1: w/ Rhy. Fig. 1, simile, till fade

Repeat and Fade

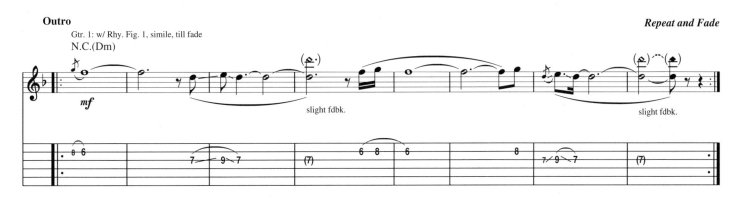

Black Sunshine

Words and Music by Rob Zombie, Shauna Reynolds, Ivan DePrume and Jay Yuenger

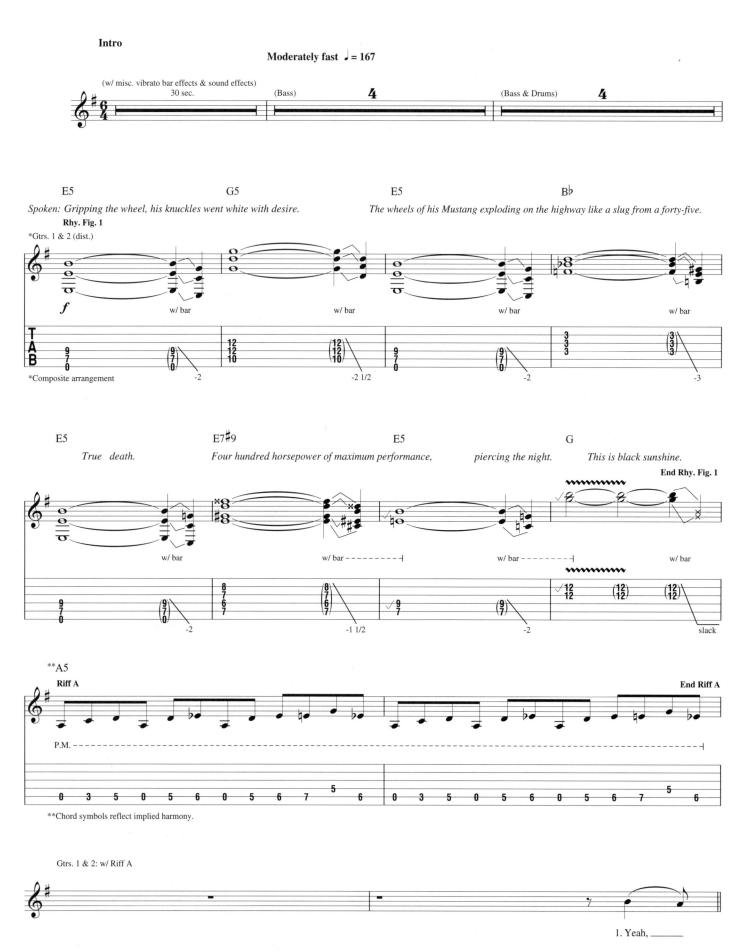

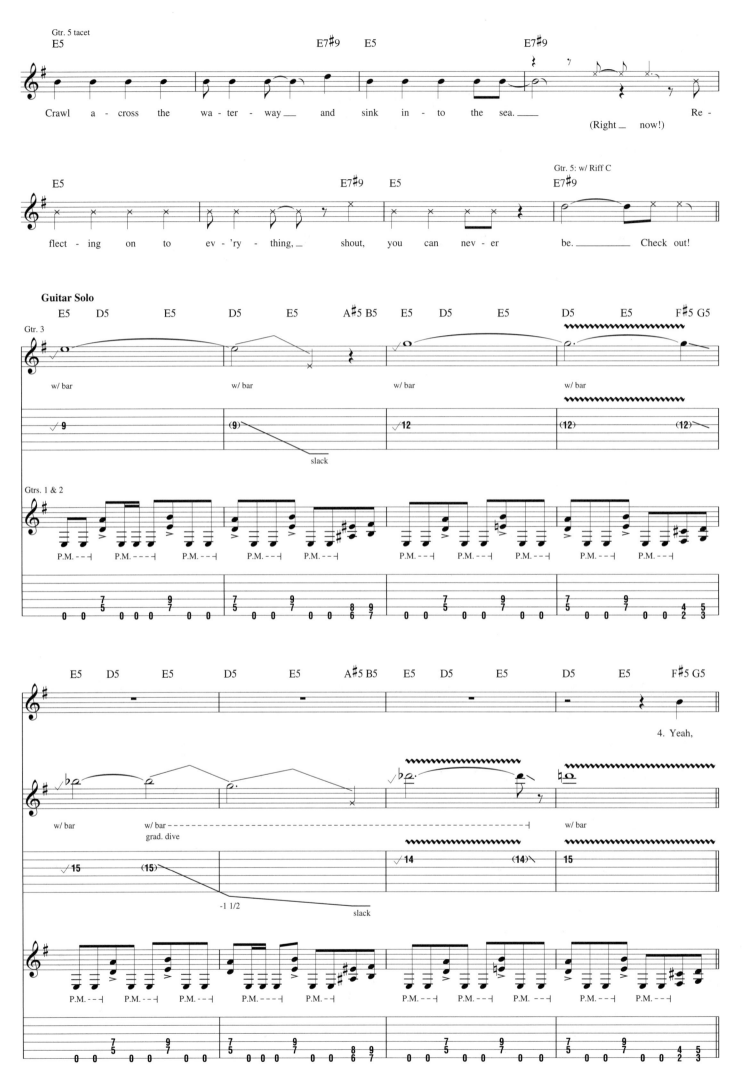

Bridge

Gtrs. 1 & 2: w/ Riff E (2 times)

E5

Stare in-to your t. v., kiss off ___ the pain. Won-der-land has fall-en, no sing, ___ no rain.

End half-time feel

Mo-men-tar-y dam-age in-to ___ the high. Drift me to the cir-cuit sky.
(Yeah, yeah, yeah, yeah, yeah, yeah, yeah, yeah.) ___

Interlude

Gtrs. 1 & 2: w/ Riff A (2 times)

A5

Gtr. 6 (dist.)

f

w/ flanger

Half-time feel

Gtr. 6

E5   F5   E5   F5

Gtrs. 1 & 2

E5   F5   E5

w/ misc. fdbk. -

P.S.

Outro

Cherub Rock

Words and Music by William Corgan

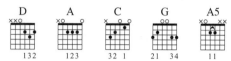

*Chord symbols reflect overall harmony.

**Composite arrangement

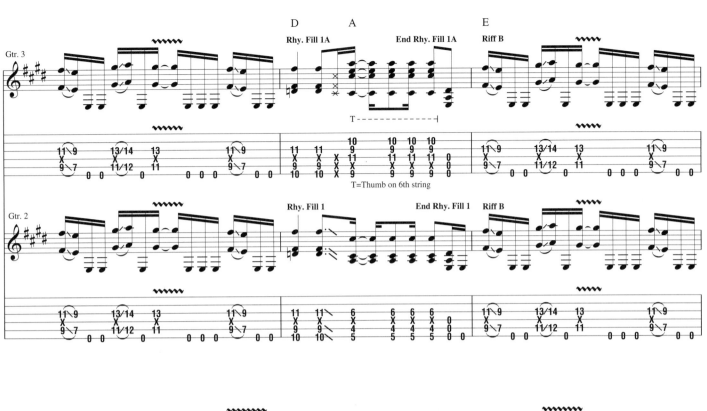

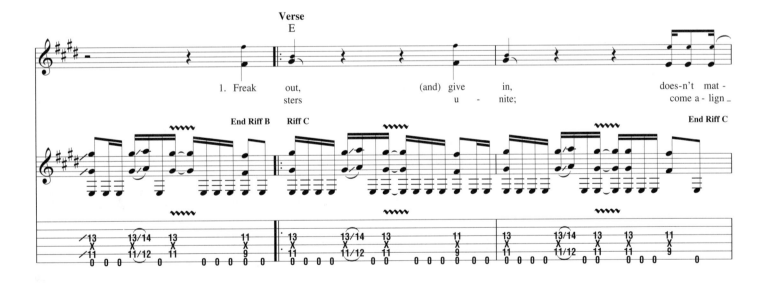

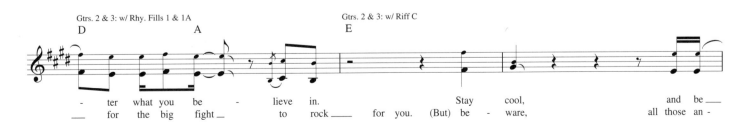

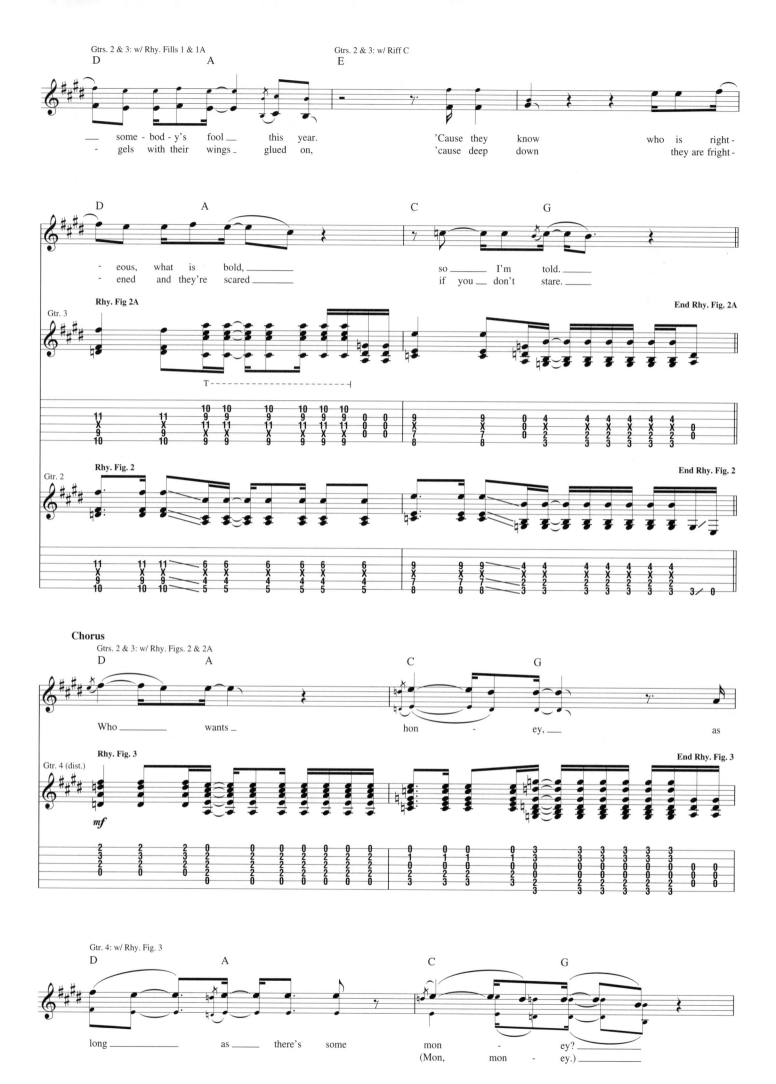

44

Tell me all _____ of your se - crets. _____ Can-not help _____ but be -

lieve _____ this __ is true. __ Tell me all _____ of your se - crets. I know, _

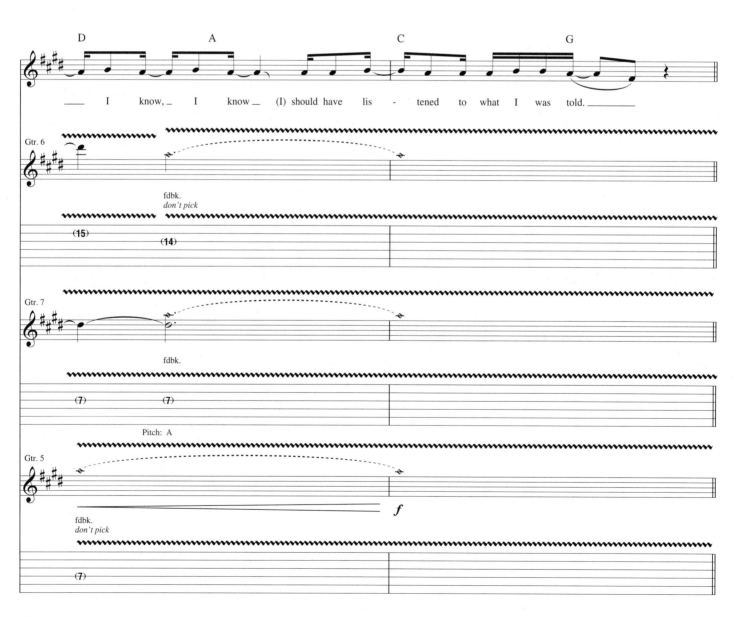

_ I know, _ I know _ (I) should have lis - tened to what I was told. _____

Chorus
Gtrs. 2 & 3: w/ Rhy. Figs. 2 & 2A (2 times)
Gtr. 4: w/ Rhy. Fig. 3 (2 times)
Gtrs. 6 & 7 tacet

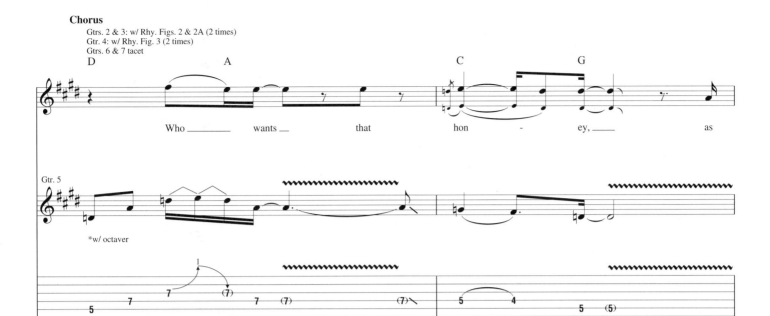

*w/ octaver

*Set for one octave above

50

Cities on Flame with Rock 'N' Roll

Words and Music by Samuel Pearlman, Donald Roeser and Albert Bouchard

Cliffs of Dover

By Eric Johnson

Cult of Personality

Words and Music by William Calhoun, Corey Glover, Muzz Skillings and Vernon Reid

(Malcom X) *Spoken: "And during the few moments that we have left... We want to talk right down to earth in a language that everybody here can easily understand."*

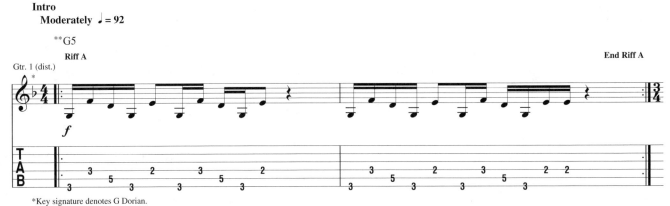

*Key signature denotes G Dorian.
**Chord symbols reflect basic harmony.

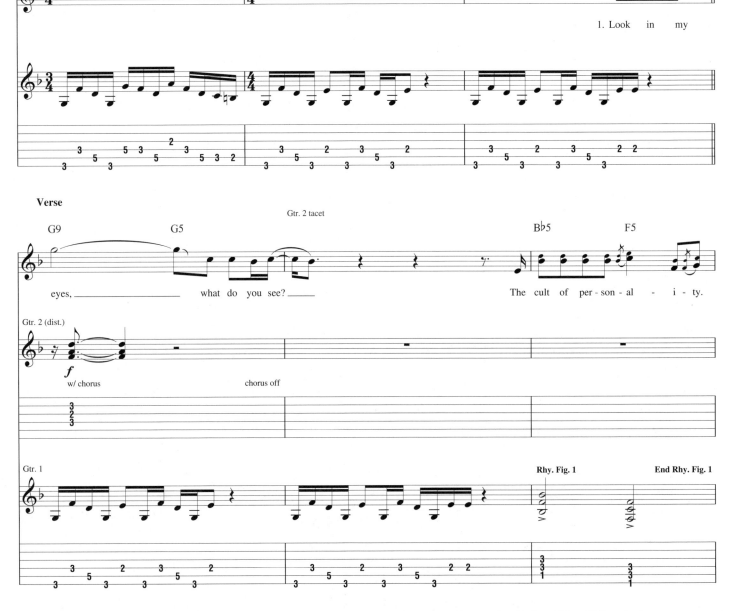

Gtr. 1: w/ Riff A (1 1/2 times)

I know your an - ger, I know your dreams. ____ I've

been ev-'ry-thing you wan - na be. ____ Oh, ____ I'm the cult of per - son - al - i - ty. ____

Gtr. 1: w/ Riff A (1 1/2 times)

Like Mus - so - li - ni an' Ken - ne - dy, ____ I'm ____ the

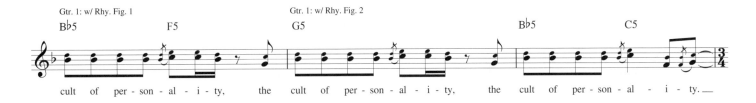

cult of per - son - al - i - ty, the cult of per - son - al - i - ty, the cult of per - son - al - i - ty. ____

Interlude

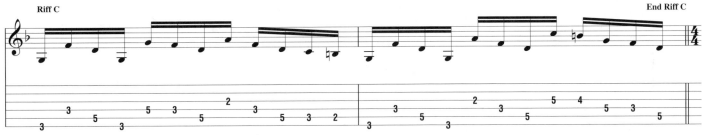

Guitar Solo

Gtr. 1 tacet

G5

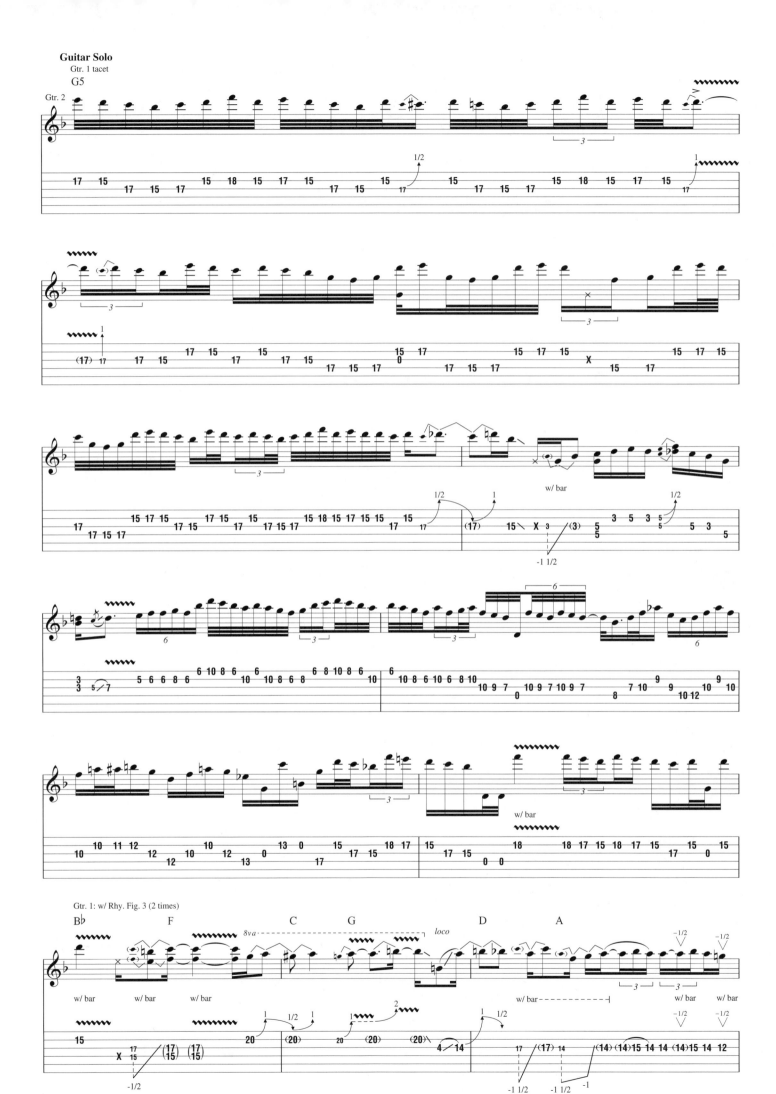

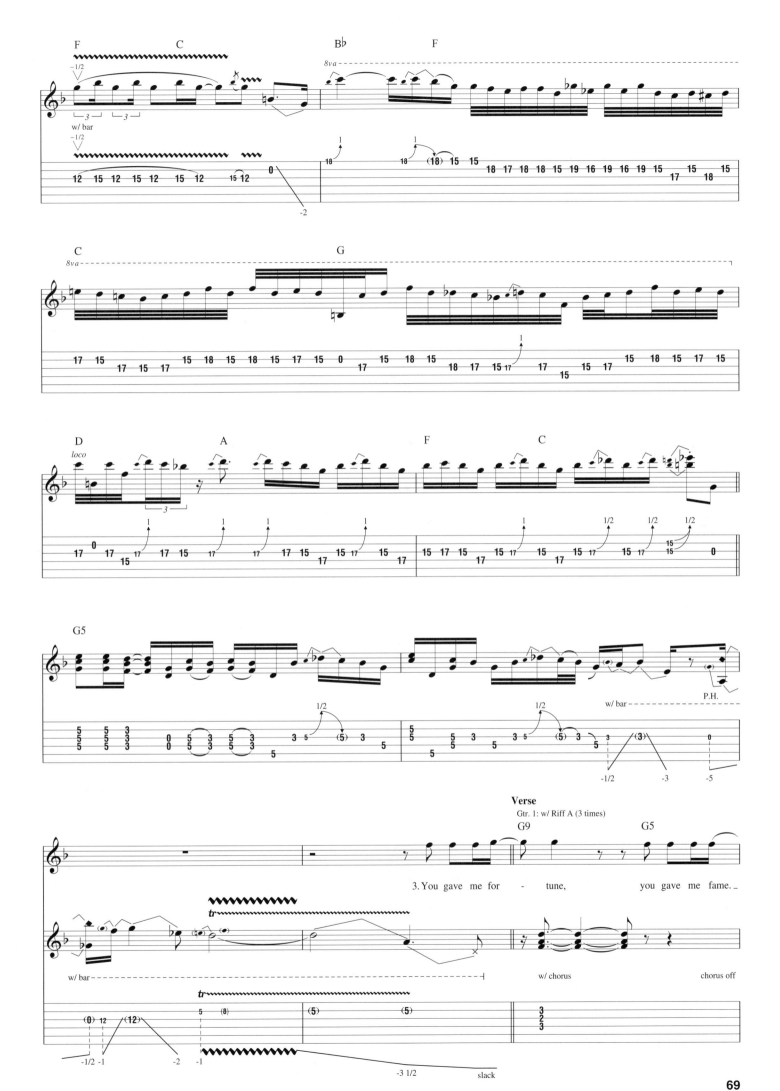

The Devil Went Down to Georgia

Words and Music by Charlie Daniels, John Thomas Crain, Jr., William Joel DiGregorio, Fred Laroy Edwards, Charles Fred Hayward and James Wainwright Marshall

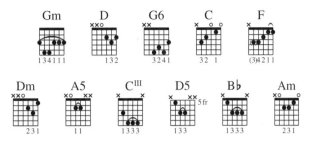

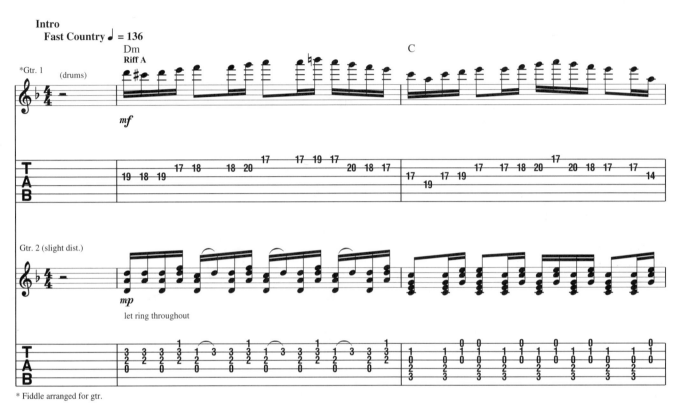

* Fiddle arranged for gtr.

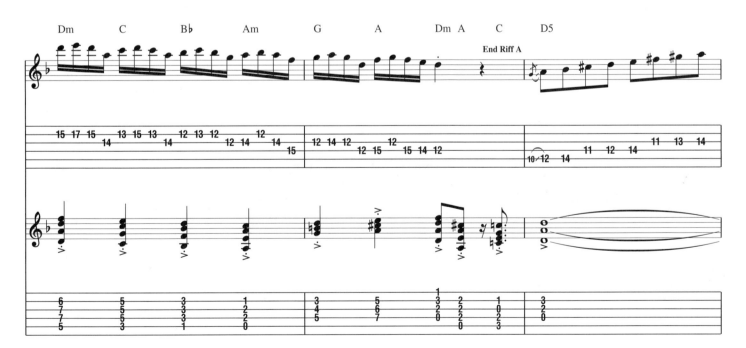

came a-cross _ this young man saw-in' on a fid-dle an' play-in' it hot. __ An' the

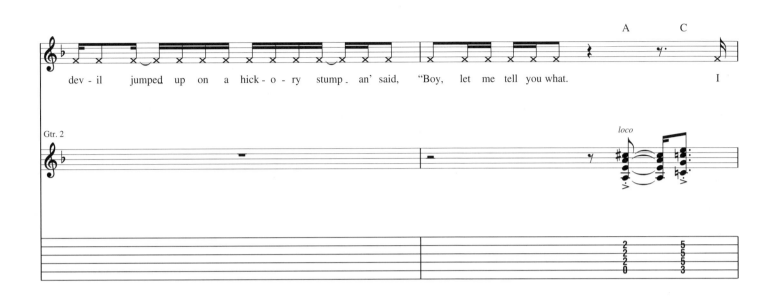

A   C

dev-il jumped up on a hick-o-ry stump _ an' said, "Boy, let me tell you what.   I

Gtr. 2

loco

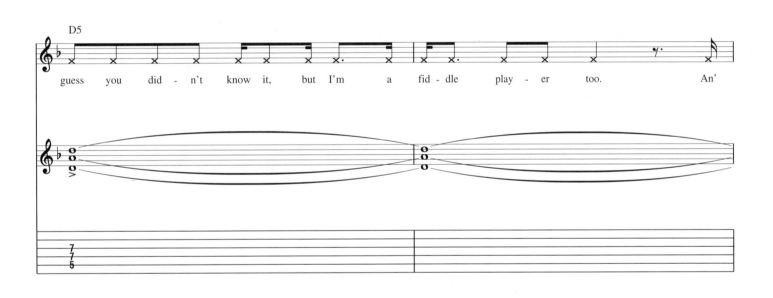

D5

guess you did-n't know it, but I'm a fid-dle play-er too.   An'

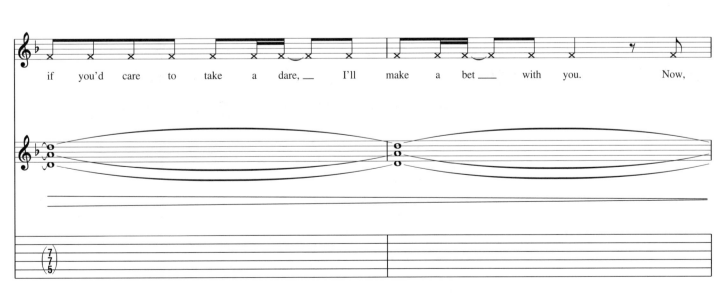

if you'd care to take a dare, __ I'll make a bet __ with you.   Now,

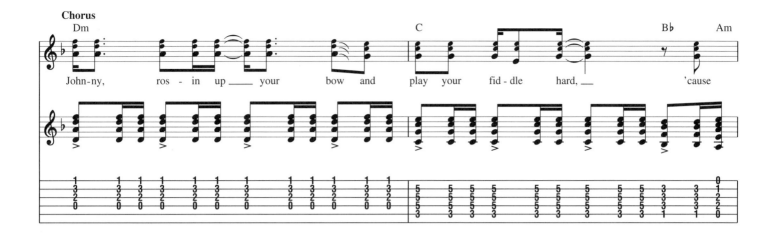

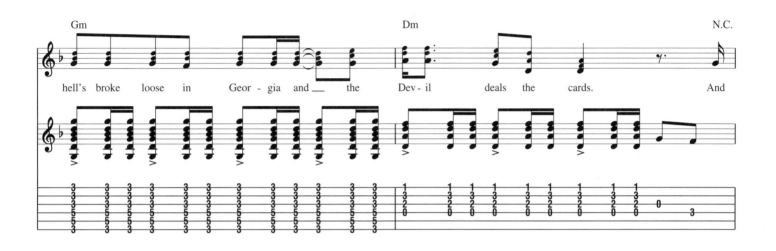

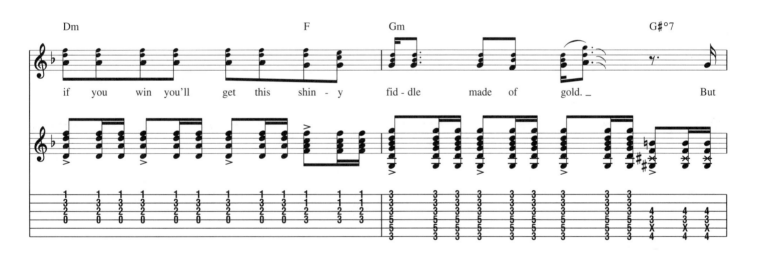

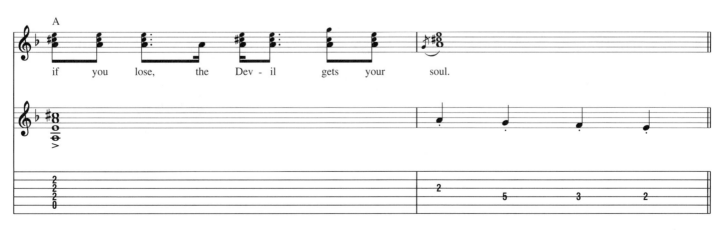

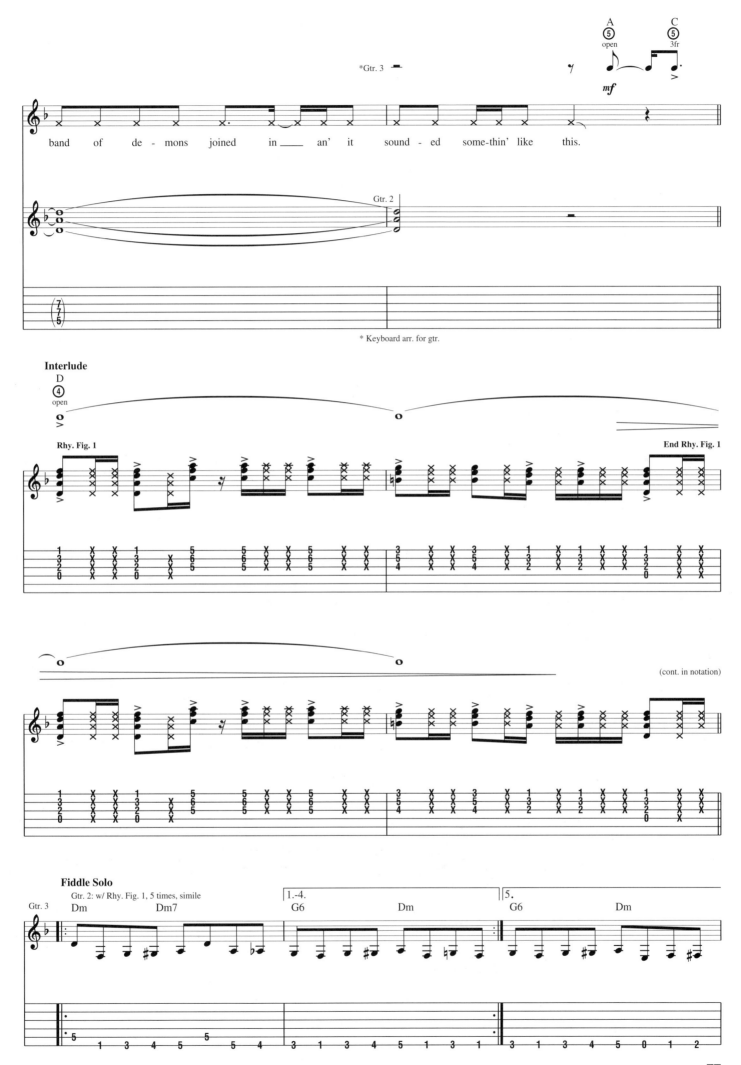

band of de - mons joined in ___ an' it sound - ed some-thin' like this.

* Keyboard arr. for gtr.

Interlude

Fiddle Solo

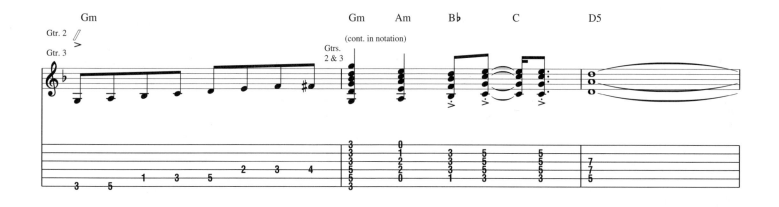

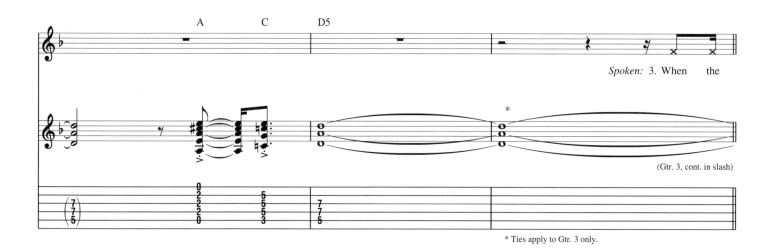

* Ties apply to Gtr. 3 only.

Verse

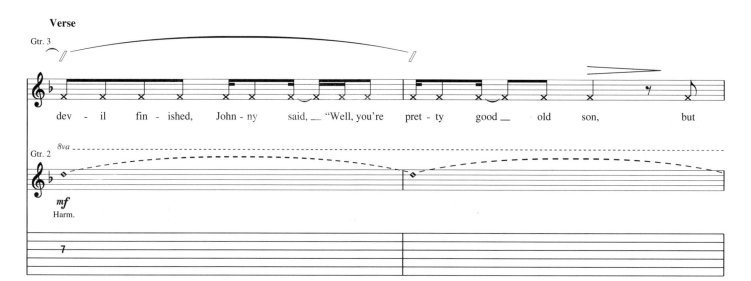

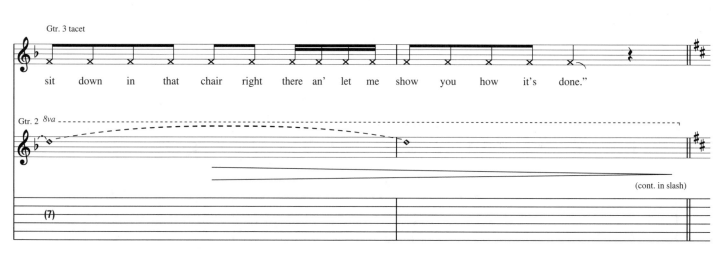

Gran-ny does your dog bite?   No,   child,   no.

Verse

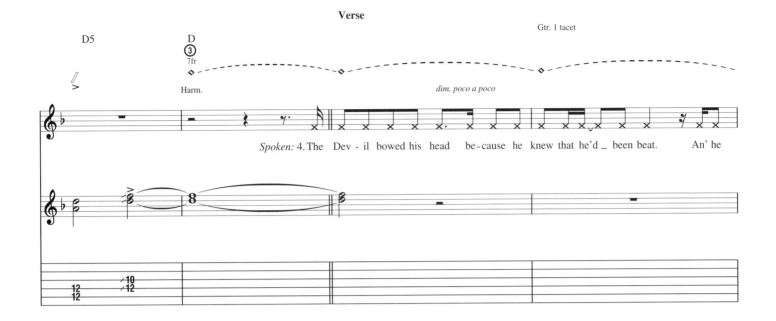

Spoken: 4. The Dev - il bowed his head be - cause he knew that he'd _ been beat. An' he

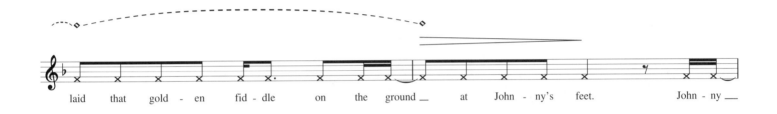

laid that gold - en fid - dle on the ground _ at John - ny's feet. John - ny _

_ said, "Dev - il, just come on back _ if you ev - er wan - na try a - gain. _ I done

D.S. al Coda

told you once, you son of a bitch, _ I'm the best that's ev - er been." _ He played.

Coda

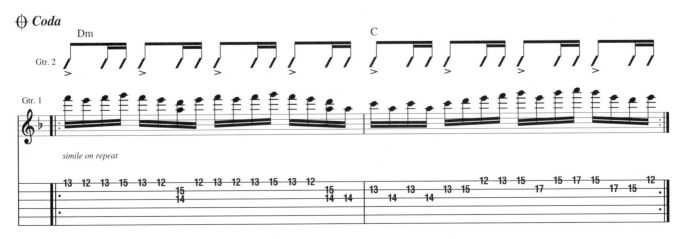

81

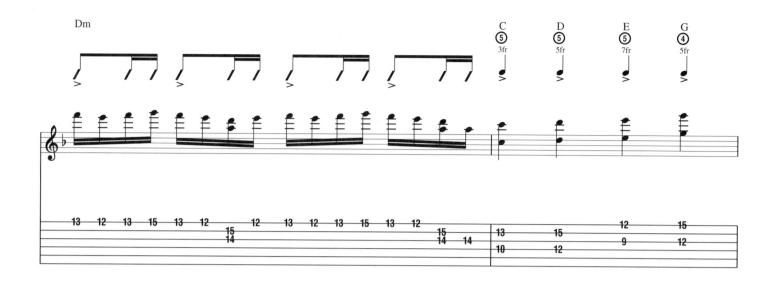

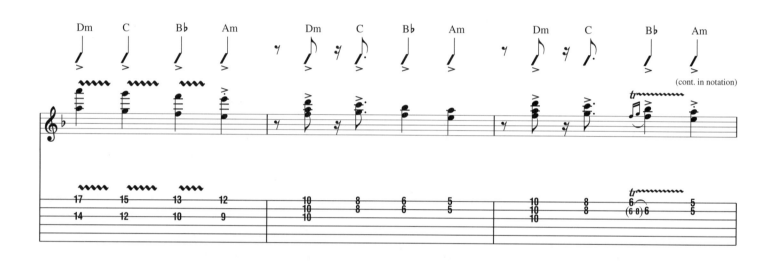

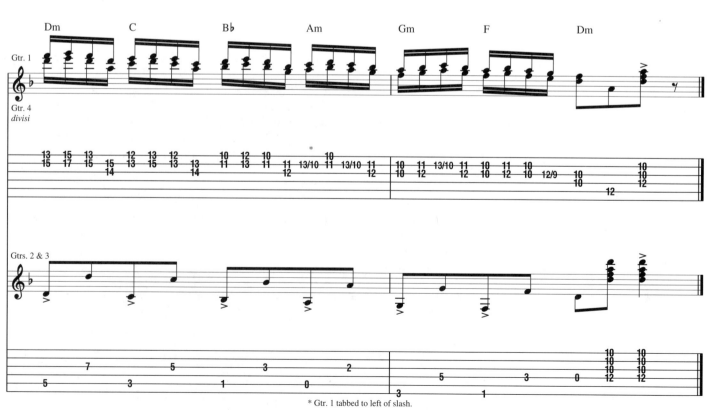

* Gtr. 1 tabbed to left of slash.

82

Even Flow

Music by Stone Gossard
Lyric by Eddie Vedder

Verse

1. Freeze   him   rest   his   head   on   a   pil - low ___ made   of   con -
2. Kneel -   ing   look-ing through the pa - per though he does-n't   know   to   read ___

w/Fill 1 (2nd time only)

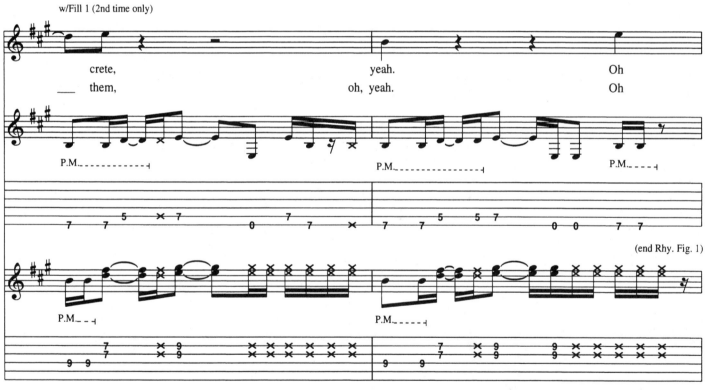

crete,   yeah.   Oh
___ them,   oh, yeah.   Oh

Fill 1

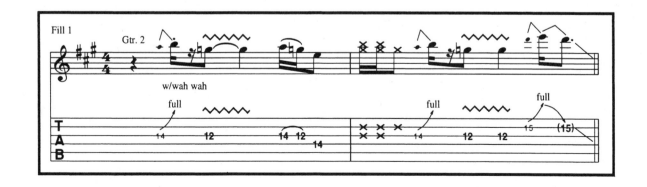

84

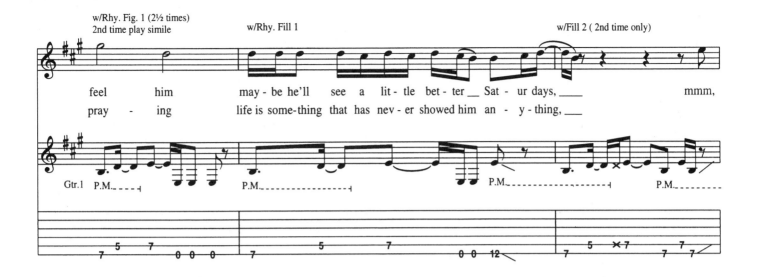

feel him   may - be he'll   see   a   lit - tle   bet - ter __ Sat - ur days, ___   mmm,
pray - ing   life is some-thing that has nev - er showed him an - y - thing, ___

yeah,   woh, ___   Hell   now   fac - es that he sees come a - gain _ ain't that fa - mil -
woh, ___   feel - ing   un - der-stands the weath - er or the win-ter's on its way. _

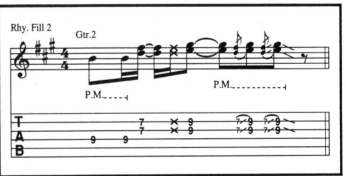

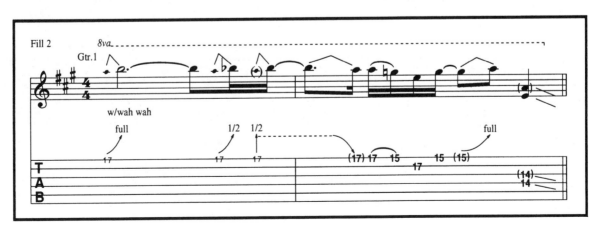

1.

Gtr. 1

Gtr. 2   w/wah wah

let ring

Chorus

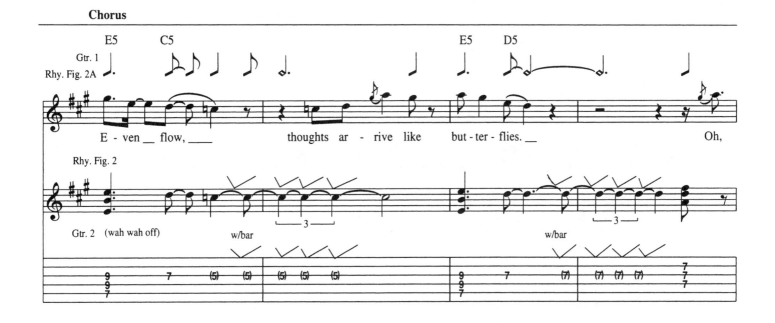

E5   C5   E5   D5

Gtr. 1
Rhy. Fig. 2A

E - ven __ flow, ____   thoughts ar - rive like   but - ter - flies. __   Oh,

Rhy. Fig. 2

Gtr. 2   (wah wah off)   w/bar   w/bar

* Simultaneously play lower note with pick and upper note with middle finger

Hit Me with Your Best Shot

Words and Music by Eddie Schwartz

3. Well, you're a

Verse

real tough cook-ie with a long his-to-ry of break-ing lit-tle hearts like the one in me. Be-fore I

*Chord symbols reflect implied harmony.

Pitch: F♯ G♯ F♯

put an-oth-er notch in my lip-stick case, you'd bet-ter make sure you put me in my place.

Pitch: F♯ G♯ F♯

Holiday in Cambodia

Words and Music by Bruce Slesinger, Darren Henley, East Bay Ray, Jello Biafra and Klaus Flouride

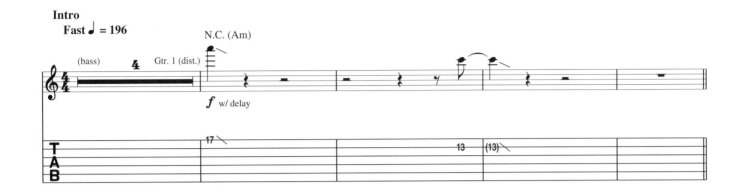

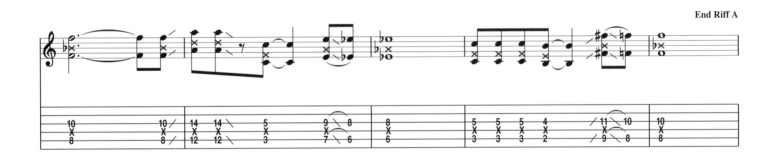

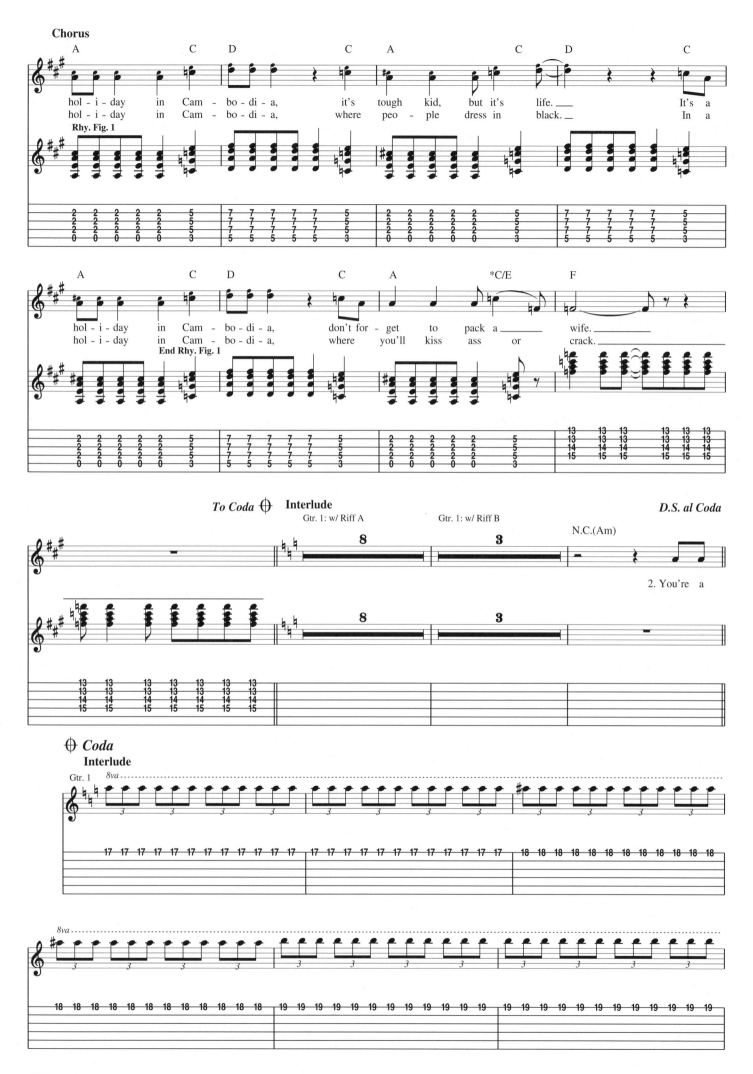

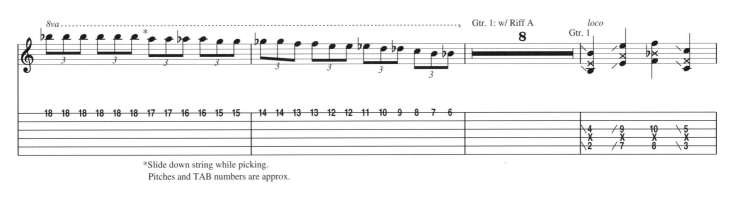

*Slide down string while picking.
Pitches and TAB numbers are approx.

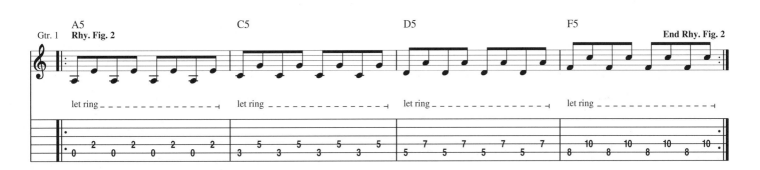

Bridge

Pol   Pot,   Pol   Pot.   Pot.   And   it's   a

*Sound effects are created by randomly running a slide up and down gtr. neck.

Outro-Chorus

hol-i-day   in   Cam-bo-di-a,   where   you'll   do   what   you're   told.   A   hol-i-day   in   Cam-

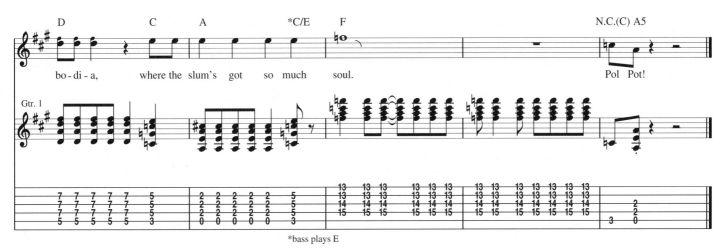

bo-di-a,   where   the   slum's   got   so   much   soul.   Pol   Pot!

*bass plays E

La Grange

Words and Music by Billy F Gibbons, Dusty Hill and Frank Lee Beard

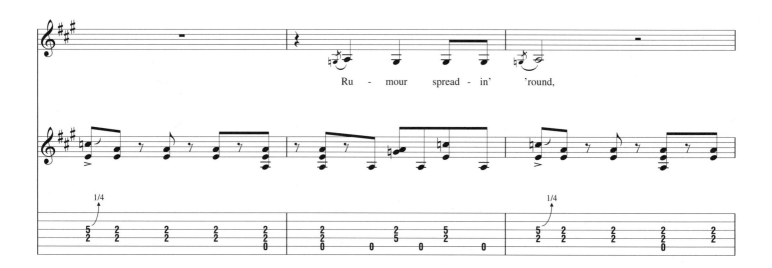

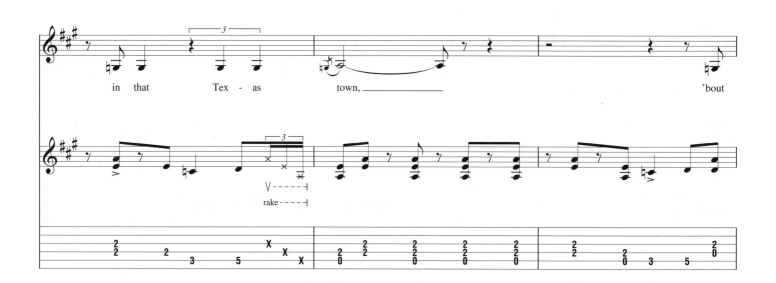

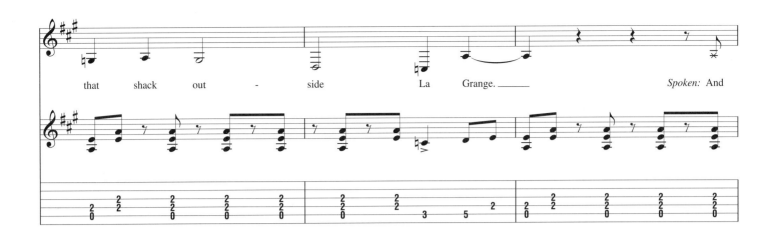

that shack out - side La Grange. _____ *Spoken:* And

you know what I'm talk - in' a - bout. Just let me know if you ___ wan - na go ___

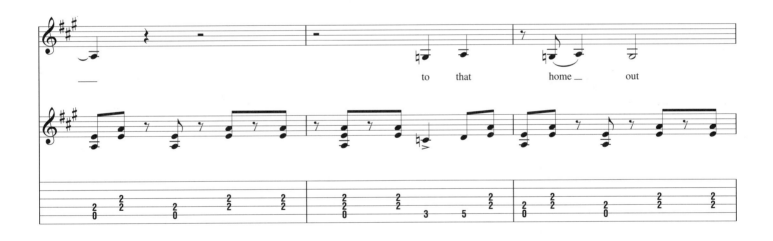

to that home ___ out

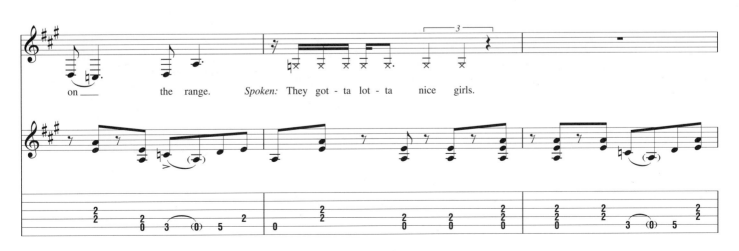

on ___ the range. *Spoken:* They got - ta lot - ta nice girls.

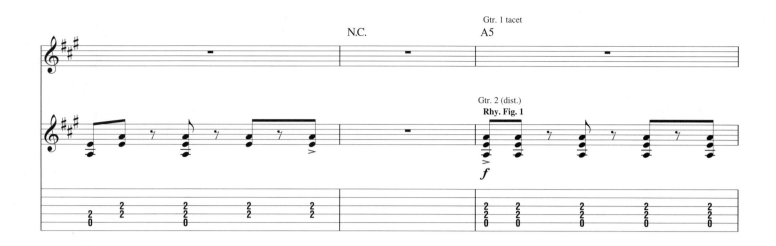

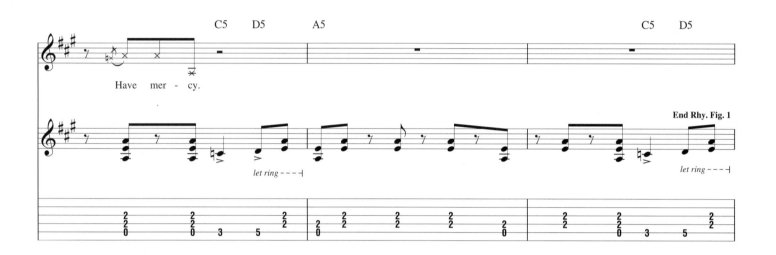

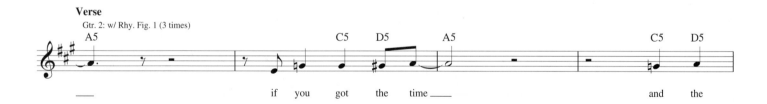

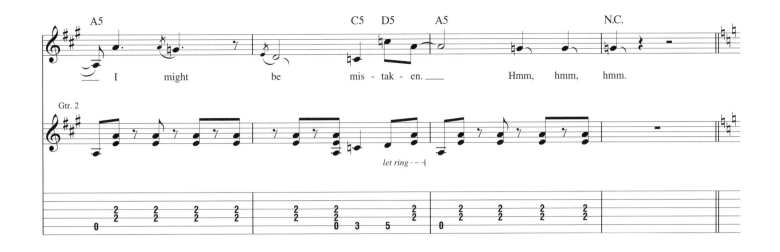

I might be mis - tak - en. ____ Hmm, hmm, hmm.

Guitar Solo

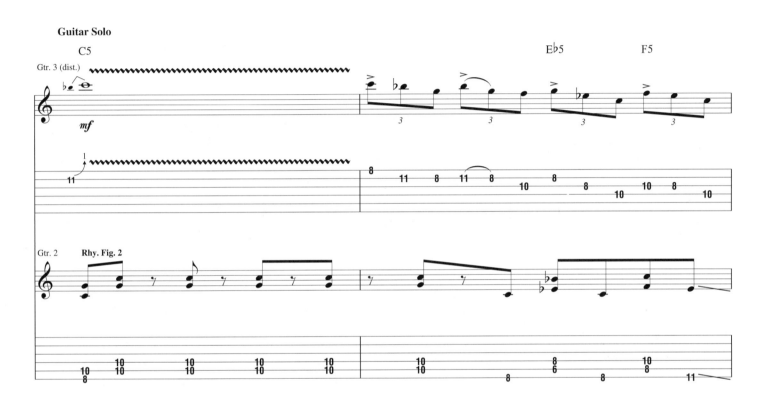

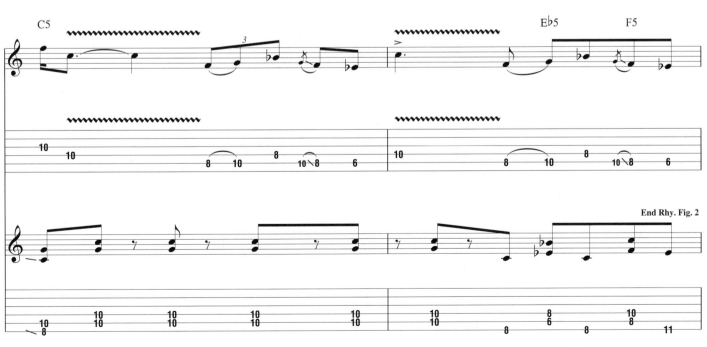

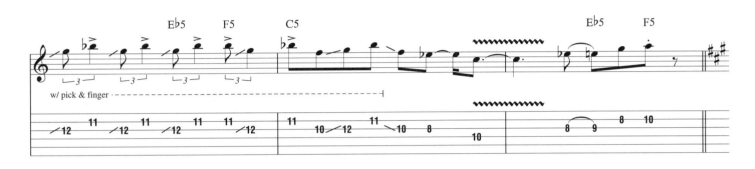

*Composite arrangement

Outro-Guitar Solo

Gtr. 1 tacet

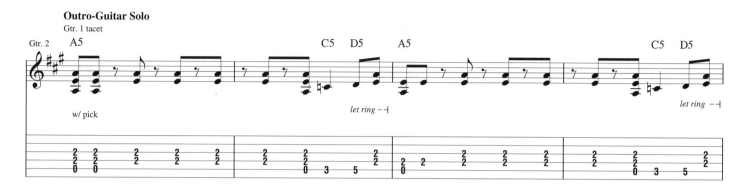

Gtr. 2: w/ Rhy. Fig. 1 (till fade)

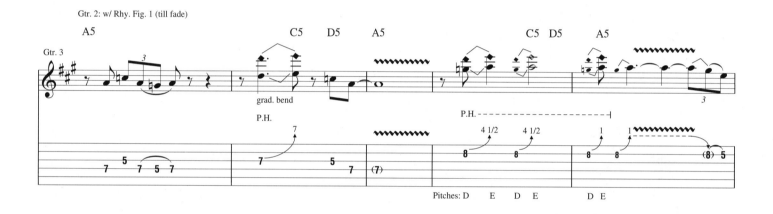

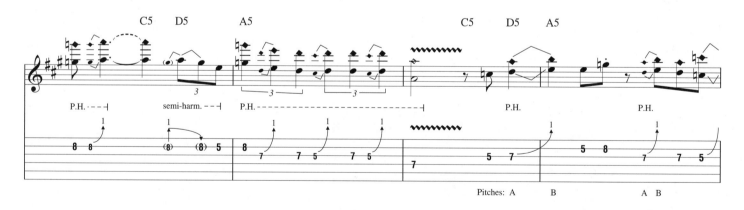

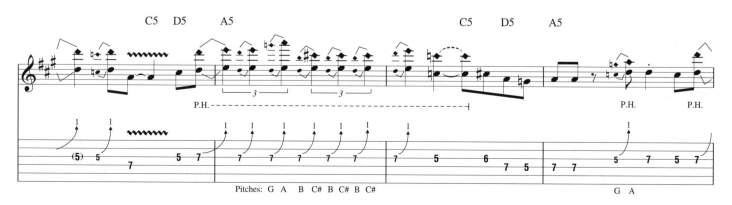

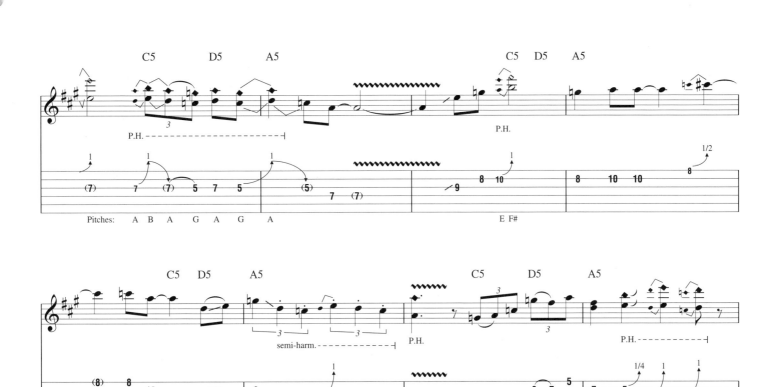

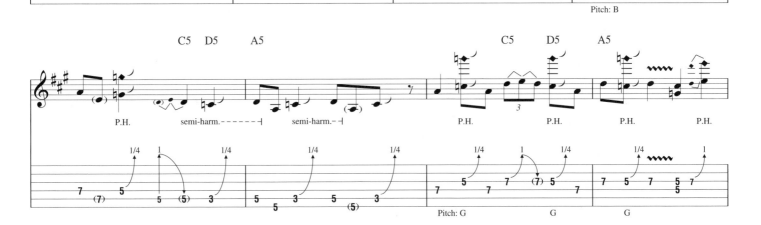

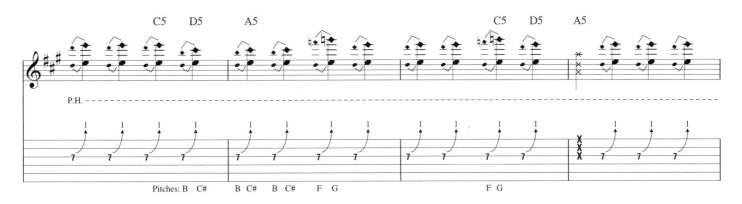

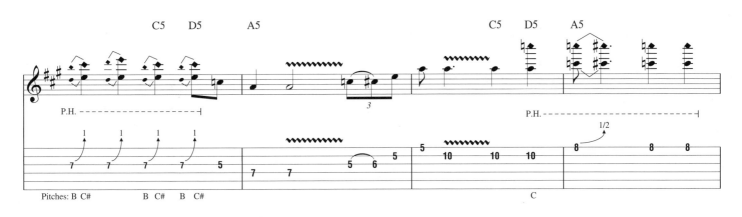

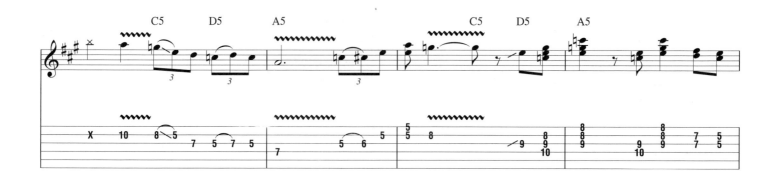

The Metal

Words and Music by Jack Black, Kyle Gass, John King and John S. Konesky

Gtr. 2: w/ Riff A

F5

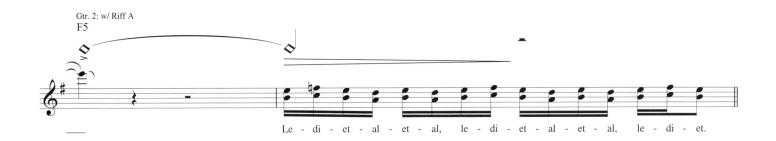

Le - di - et - al - et - al, le - di - et - al - et - al, le - di - et.

Bridge

Gtrs. 1 & 2 tacet

*Em   Dadd$\frac{2}{4}$ Cadd9   D$^6_9$sus4

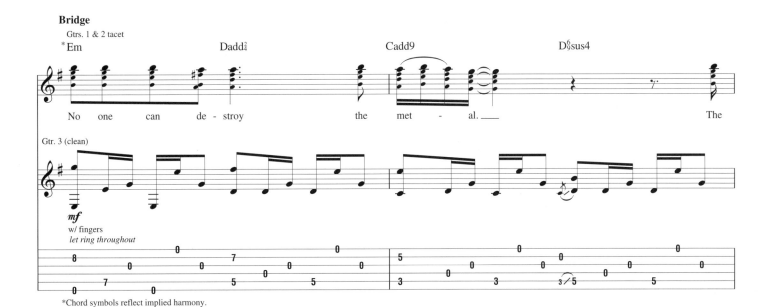

No one can de - stroy the met - al. ___ The

Gtr. 3 (clean)

mf

w/ fingers

let ring throughout

*Chord symbols reflect implied harmony.

Em   Dadd$\frac{2}{4}$ Cadd9   D   C   Bm   C

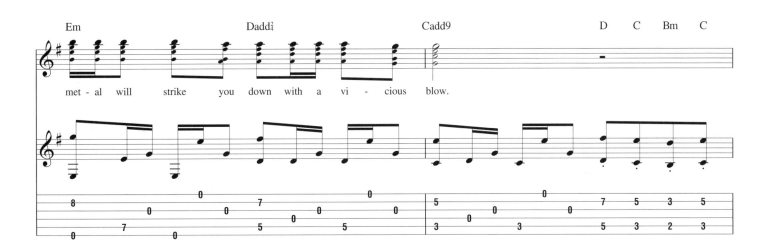

met - al will strike you down with a vi - cious blow.

Am7   Bm(add$\flat$$^4_6$)   Em

We are the van - quished foes of the met - al. ___ We

tried to win, for why, we do not know.

Verse

Gtr. 1: w/ Rhy. Fig. 1 (5 times)
Gtr. 3 tacet

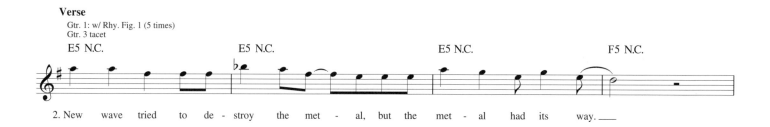

E5 N.C.　　　　　E5 N.C.　　　　　E5 N.C.　　　　　F5 N.C.

2. New wave tried to de - stroy the met - al, but the met - al had its way. ___

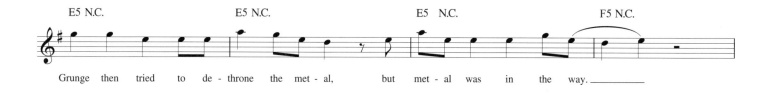

E5 N.C.　　　　　E5 N.C.　　　　　E5 N.C.　　　　　F5 N.C.

Grunge then tried to de - throne the met - al, but met - al was in the way. ___

E5 N.C.　　　　　E5 N.C.　　　　　E5 N.C.　　　　　F5 N.C.

Punk rock tried to de - stroy ___ the met - al, but met - al was much too strong.

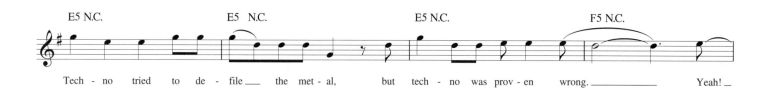

E5 N.C.　　　　　E5 N.C.　　　　　E5 N.C.　　　　　F5 N.C.

Tech - no tried to de - file ___ the met - al, but tech - no was prov - en wrong. _____ Yeah! ___

E5 N.C.　　　　　E5 N.C.　　　　　E5 N.C.　　　　　F5 N.C.

___ Met - al　*(met - al, met - al),　　　it comes from hell ___
　　　　　　　*Echo repeats

Outro

Gtr. 1 tacet

N.C.

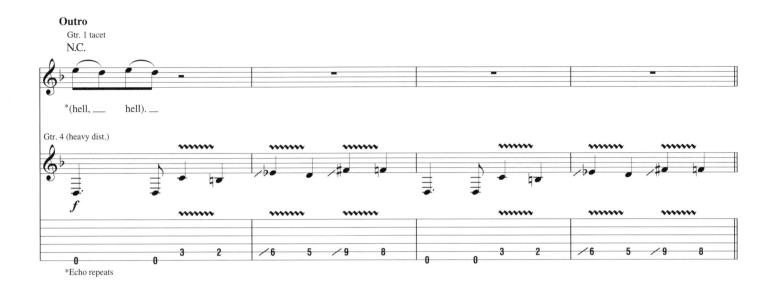

*(hell, ___ hell). ___

Gtr. 4 (heavy dist.)

*Echo repeats

Half-time feel

2nd time, end half-time feel

Gtrs. 4 & 5 (heavy dist.)

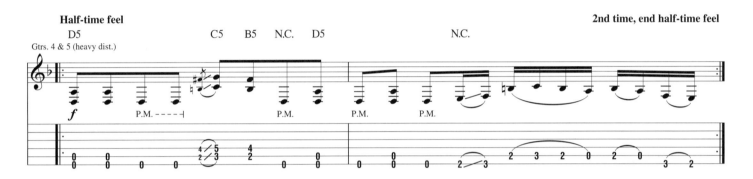

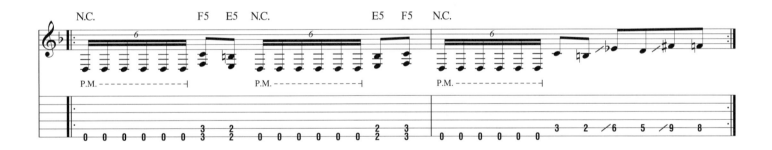

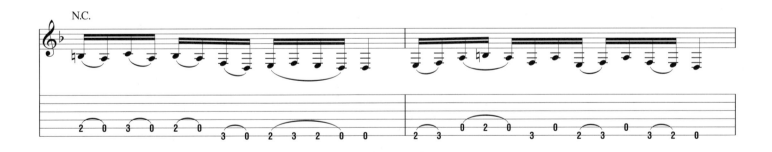

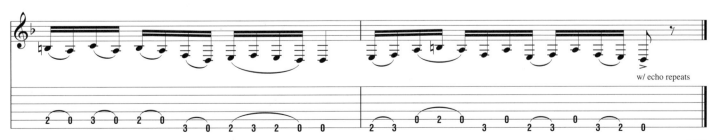

w/ echo repeats

Mississippi Queen

Words and Music by Leslie West, Felix Pappalardi, Corky Laing and David Rea

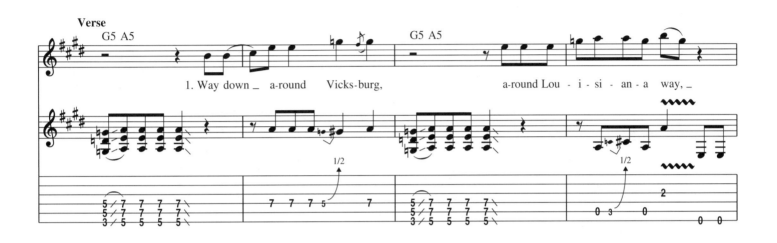

Verse

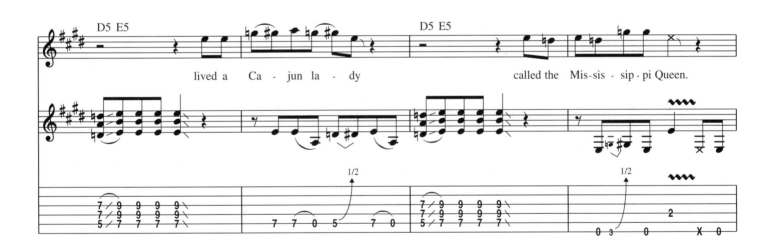

rest of them dudes was a' get-tin' their kicks; bud-dy, beg your par-don I was get-tin' mine.

End Rhy. Fig. 1

* Top note vib. only.

Chorus

Gtr. 1: w/ Rhy. Fig .1

Mis - sis-sip-pi Queen, __ if you know ___what I mean. _

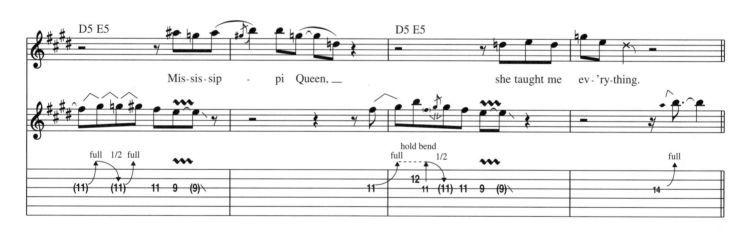

Mis-sis-sip - pi Queen, __ she taught me ev-'ry-thing.

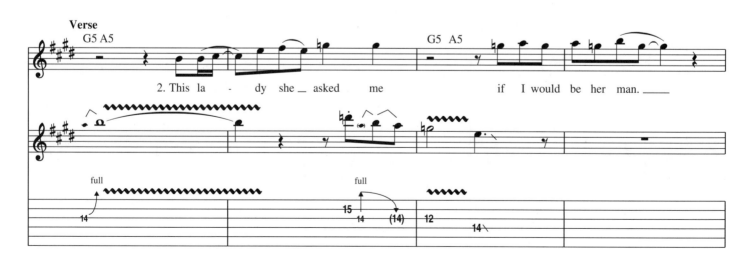

Verse

2. This la - dy she _ asked me if I would be her man. ____

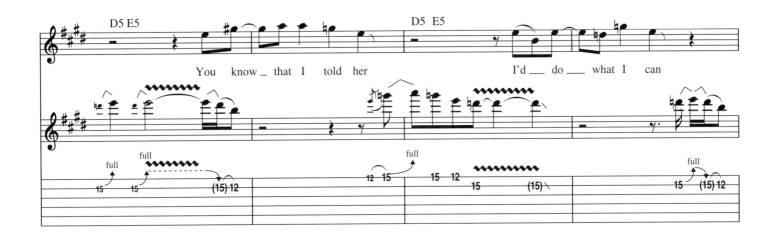

You know __ that I told her __ I'd __ do __ what I can

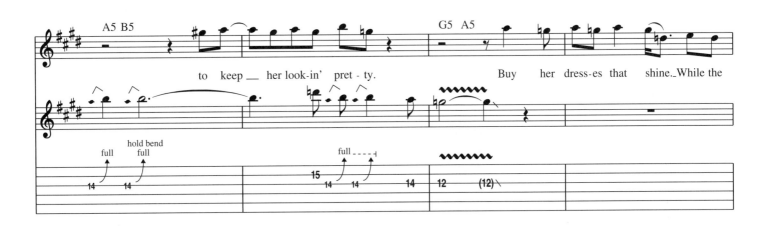

to keep __ her look-in' pret - ty. Buy her dress-es that shine. __ While the

rest of them dudes was a' mak-in' their bread; bud-dy, beg your par-don I was los - in' mine.

Guitar Solo

Gtr. 1: w/ Rhy. Fig. 1, 1st 23 meas. only

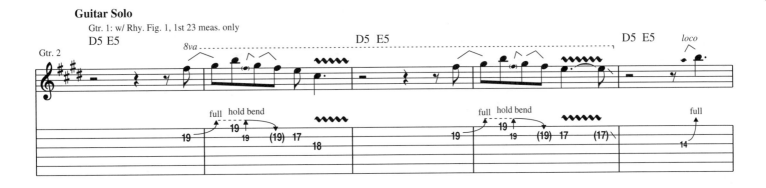

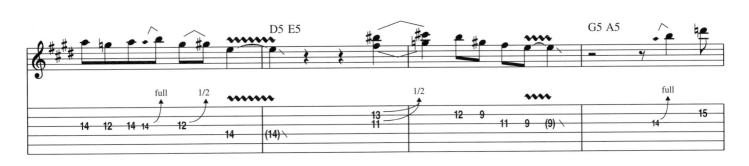

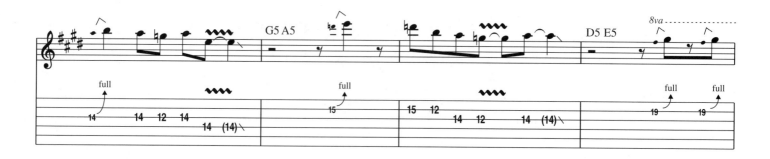

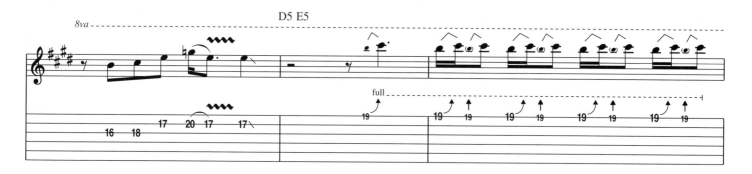

You know ___ she was a danc - er, ___ she moved ___ bet - ter on wine. While the

rest of them ___ dudes ___ was ___ get-tin' their kicks; broth-er, beg your par-don I was get-tin' mine. ___

Hey, _____ Mis - sis - sip - pi Queen. ___

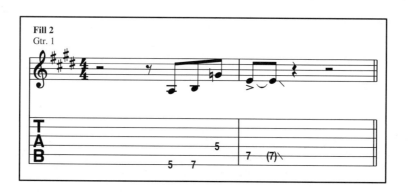

My Name Is Jonas

Words and Music by Rivers Cuomo, Jason Cropper and Patrick Wilson

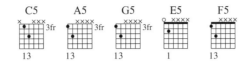

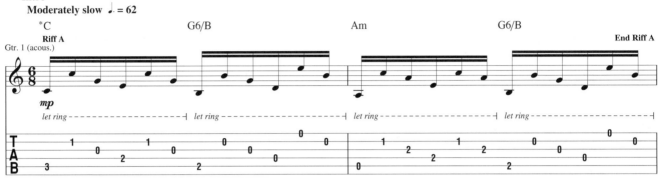

*Chord symbols reflect implied harmony.

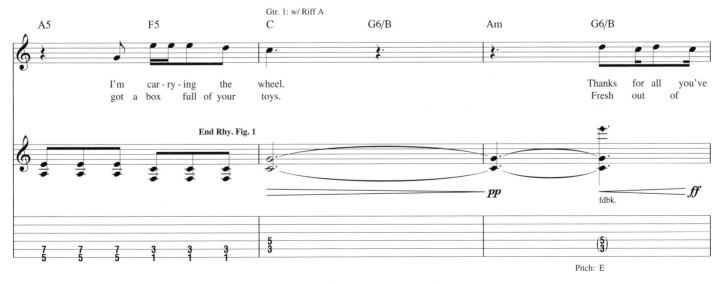

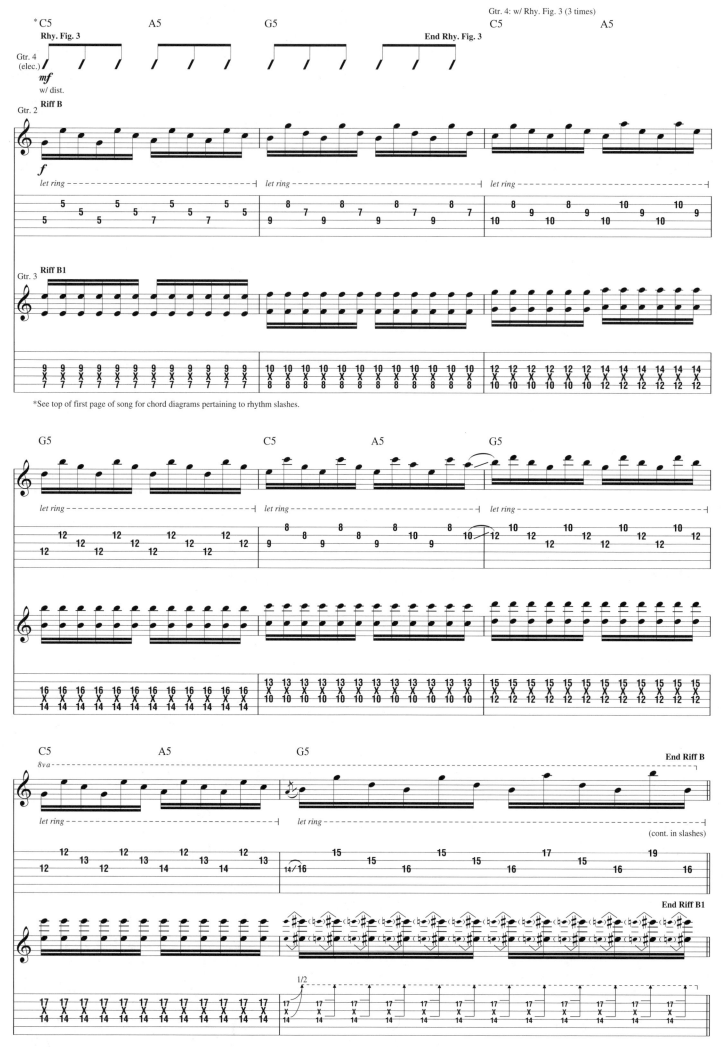

*See top of first page of song for chord diagrams pertaining to rhythm slashes.

The Number of the Beast

Words and Music by Steven Harris

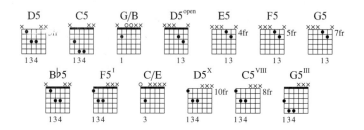

Spoken: *Woe to you, oh, Earth and Sea,*
For the Devil sends the beast with wrath,
Because he knows the time is short...
Let him who hath understanding
Reckon the number of the beast,
For it is a human number.
Its number is six hundred and sixty six.

- Revelations Ch. 13 v. 8

Intro
Fast Rock ♩ = 195

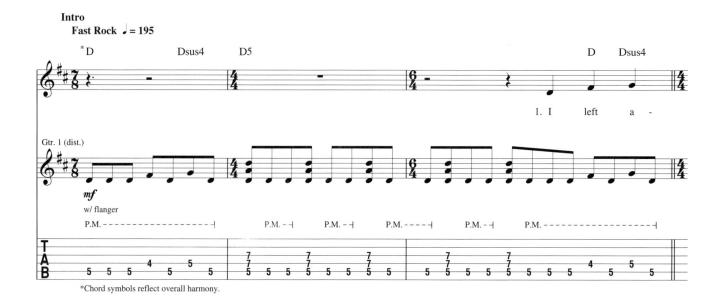

*Chord symbols reflect overall harmony.

I need-ed time to ___ think, to get the mem-'ries

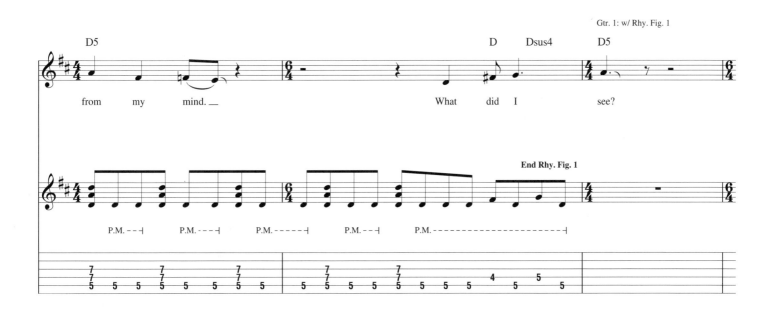

from my mind. ___ What did I see?

Can I ___ be-lieve ___ that what I saw that ___ night

was real and not just fan-ta-sy? ___ 2. Just what I

Verse

Gtr. 1: W/ Rhy. Fig. 1 (1 5/8 times)

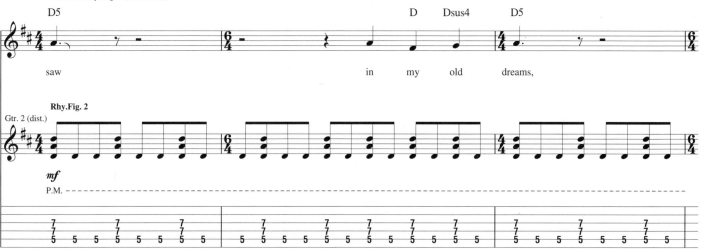

saw   in   my   old   dreams,

Rhy.Fig. 2

Gtr. 2 (dist.)

mf

P.M. --

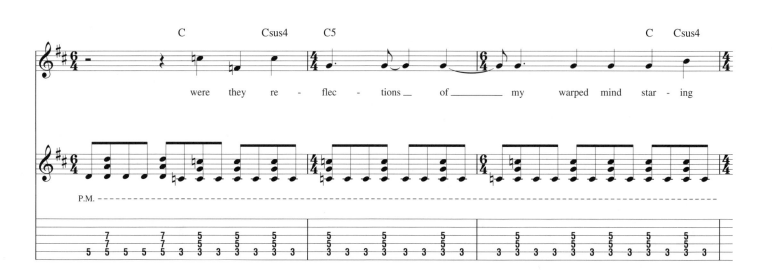

were they re - flec - tions _____ of _____ my warped mind star - ing

P.M. --

Gtr. 2: w/ Rhy. Fig. 2 (1st 7 meas.)

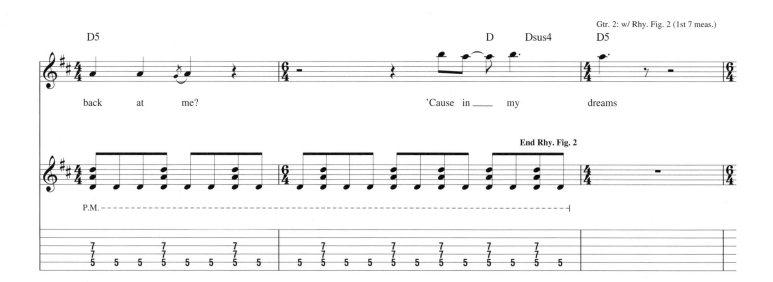

back   at   me?   'Cause in _____ my   dreams

End Rhy. Fig. 2

P.M. --

it's al - ways there,   the e - vil face that __ twists __

C   Csus4   D5   D

— my mind and brings me to de - spair.   Yeah! —

Rhy. Fig. 3
*Gtrs. 1 & 2

Gtr. 1

P.M. ---| P.M. -------------------| P.M. -| P.M. -| P.M. -----| P.M. -|

*Composite arrangement

Interlude

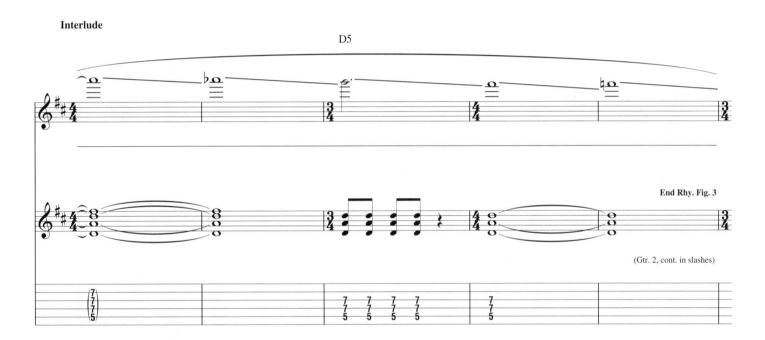

D5

End Rhy. Fig. 3

(Gtr. 2, cont. in slashes)

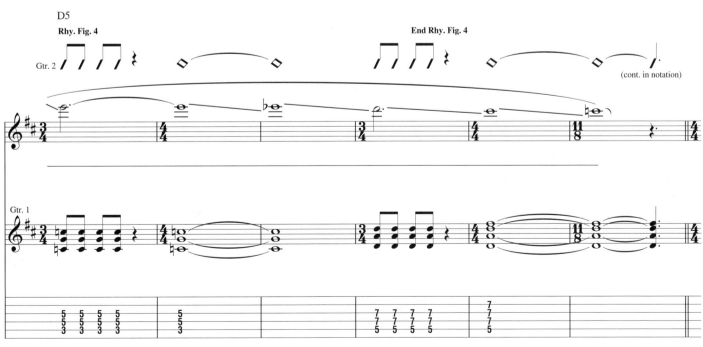

D5
Rhy. Fig. 4   End Rhy. Fig. 4

Gtr. 2   (cont. in notation)

Gtr. 1

Chorus

six, six, _____ the num - ber of ___ the beast. __

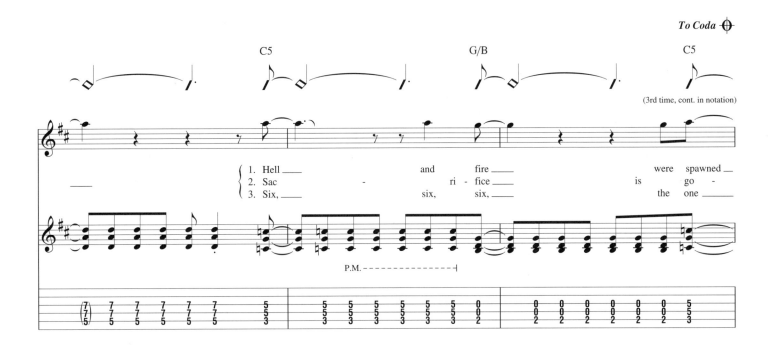

To Coda ⊕

(3rd time, cont. in notation)

1. Hell ___ and fire ___ were spawned __
2. Sac - ri - fice ___ is go -
3. Six, ___ six, six, ___ the one ___

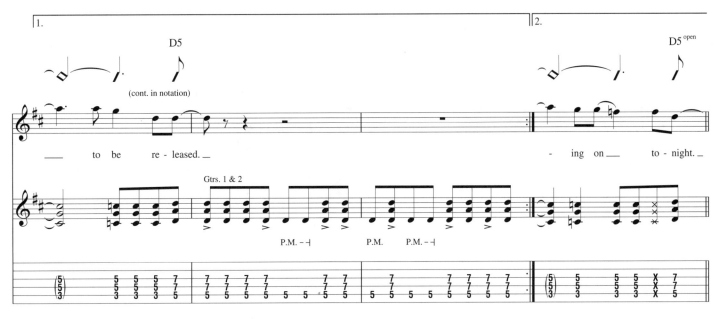

1.
___ to be re - leased. __

2.
- ing on ___ to - night. __

Interlude

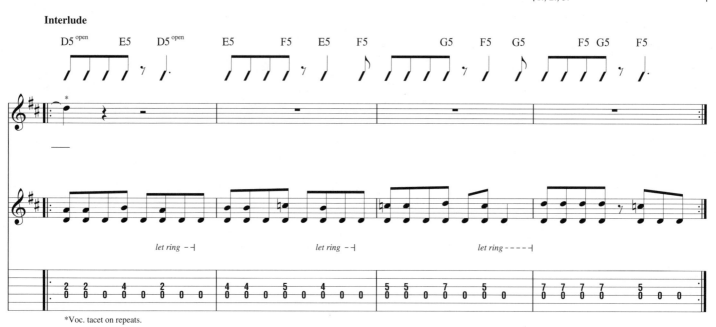

*Voc. tacet on repeats.

4.

Guitar Solo

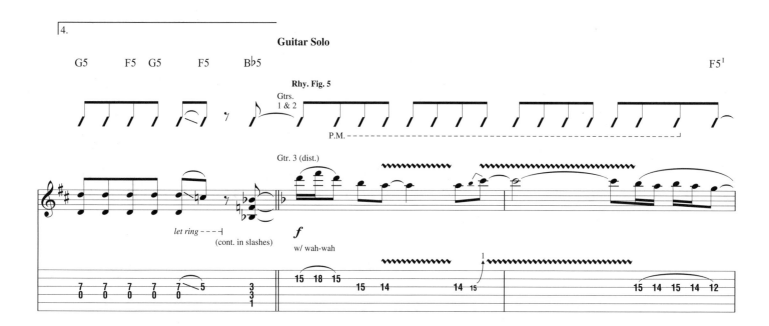

Gtrs. 1 & 2: w/ Rhy. Fig. 5 (2 times)

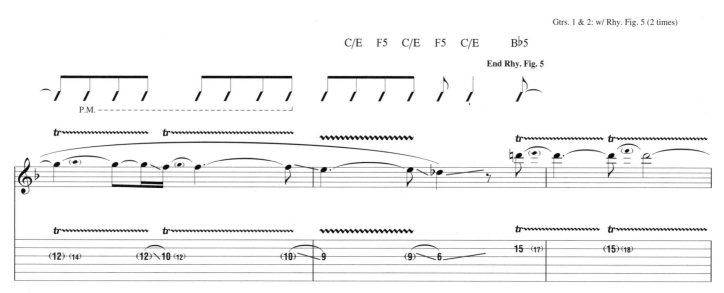

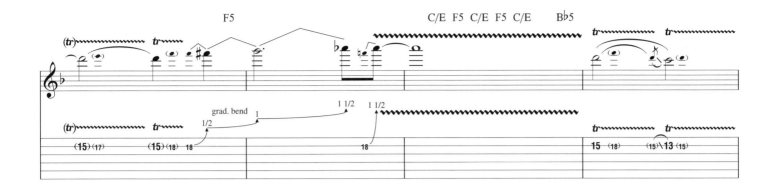

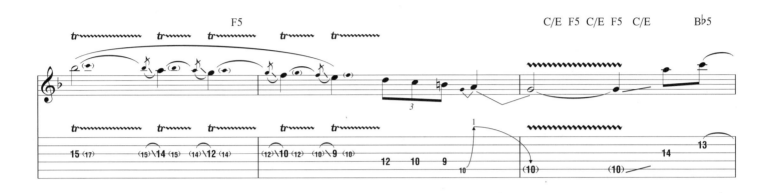

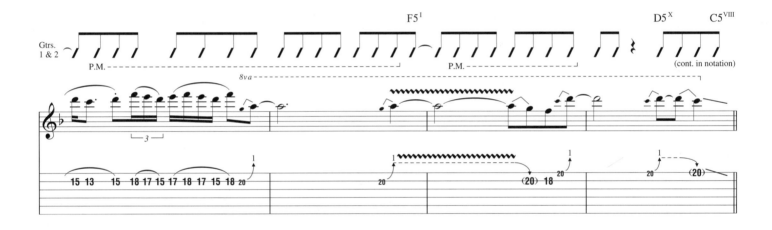

Interlude

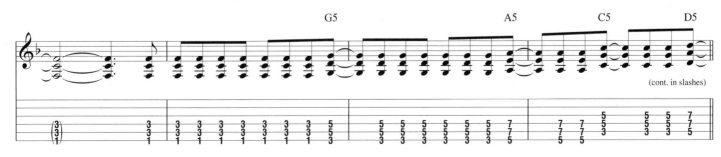

Guitar Solo

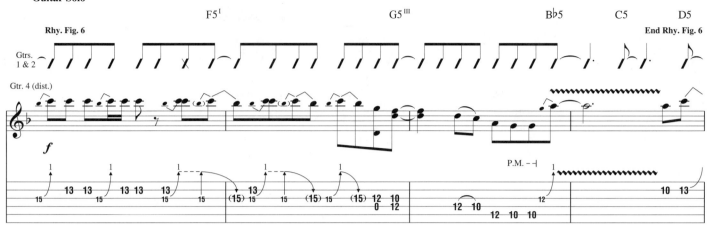

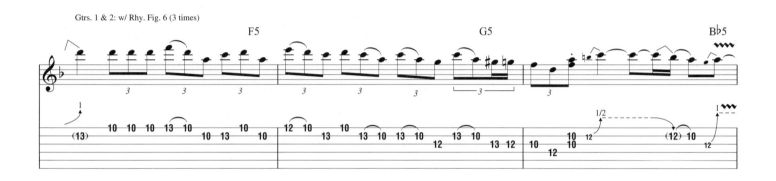

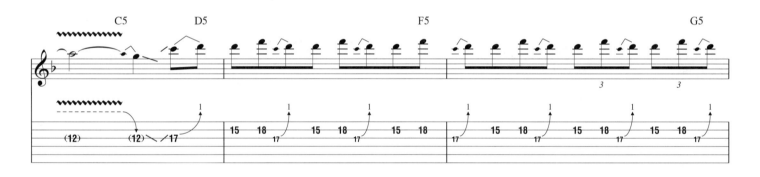

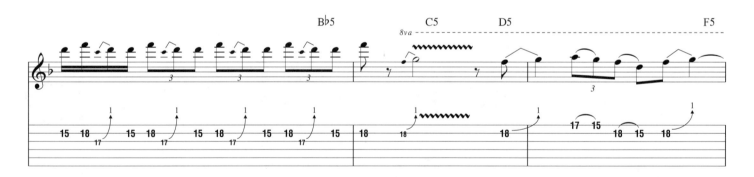

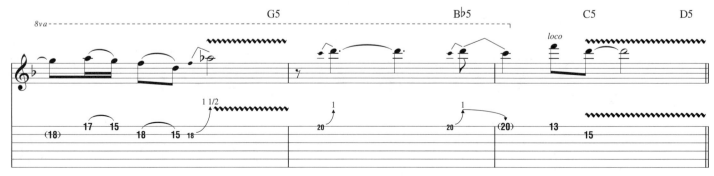

Interlude

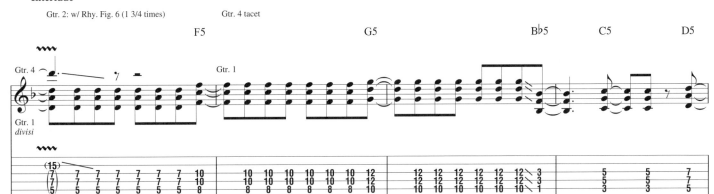

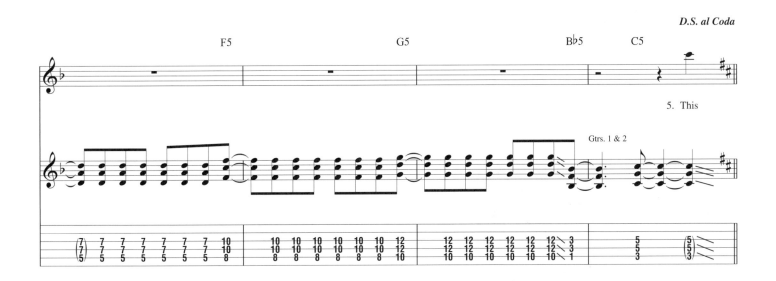

D.S. al Coda

5. This

Coda

for you and   me.   6. I'm   com-ing

Verse

Gtr. 1 : w/ Rhy. Fig. 1 (1 7/8 times)
Gtr. 2: w/ Rhy. Fig. 2 (1 7/8 times)

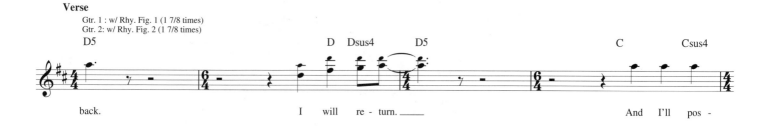

back.   I will re - turn. _____   And I'll pos -

sess your __ bod - y and I'll make you burn.   I have the

fire.   I have the force.   I have the

pow - er to _____ make my e - vil take its course.

Outro

Gtr. 2: w/ Rhy. Fig. 3

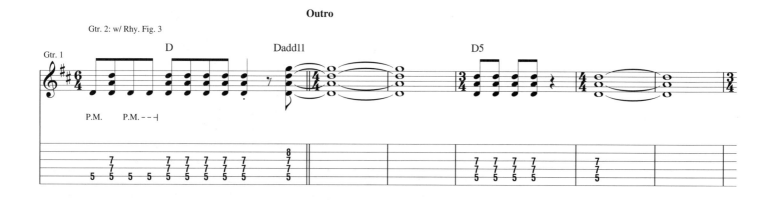

Gtr. 2: w/ Rhy. Fig. 4

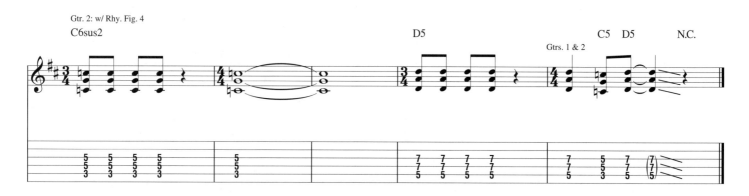

Paint It, Black

Words and Music by Mick Jagger and Keith Richards

CHORDS USED IN THIS SONG:

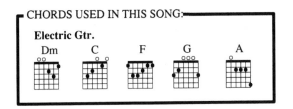

CHORDS USED IN THIS SONG:

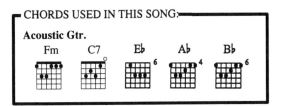

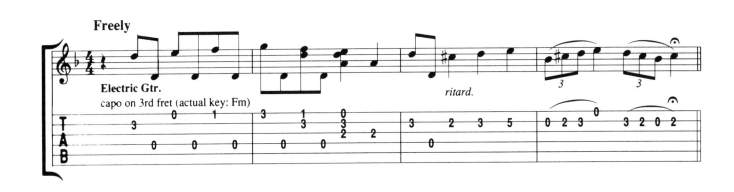

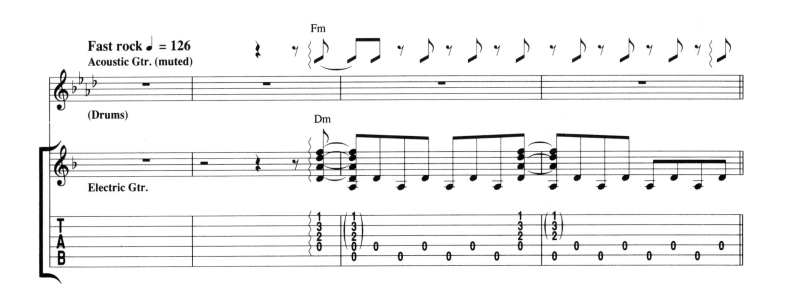

Pattern A continues

140

142

fly - ing high in the sky. I wan - na see it

paint - ed, paint - ed, paint - ed, paint - ed black, yeah. ___

Ah. _____

trem.

Repeat ad lib. overdubbed Gtr.
and fade

Ah. _____

Overdubbed Electric Gtr.

Paranoid

Words and Music by Anthony Iommi, John Osbourne, William Ward and Terence Butler

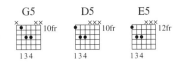

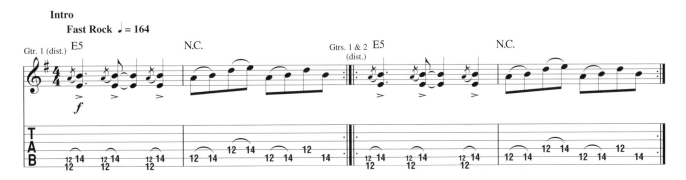

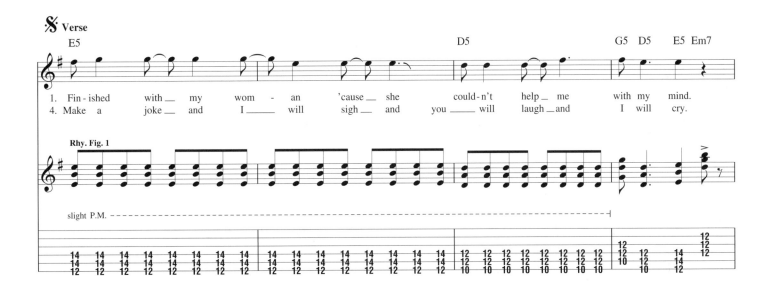

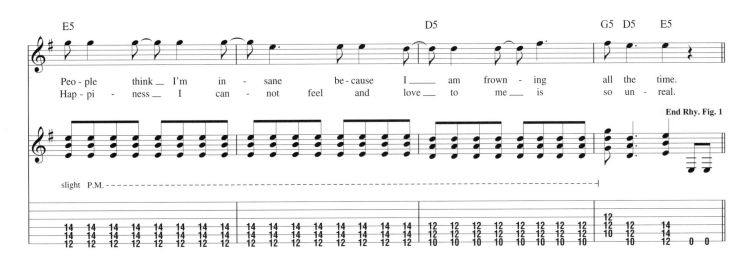

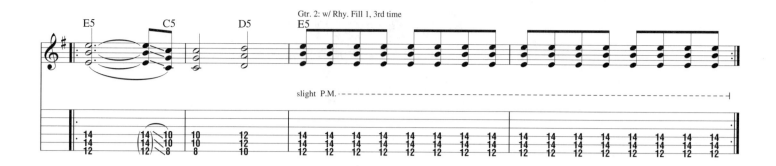

Verse

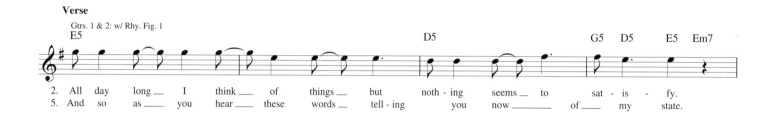

2. All day long ___ I think ___ of things ___ but noth-ing seems ___ to sat - is - fy.
5. And so as ___ you hear ___ these words ___ tell - ing you now _____ of ___ my state.

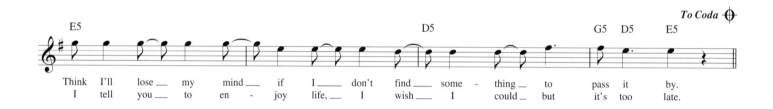

Think I'll lose ___ my mind ___ if I ___ don't find ___ some - thing ___ to pass it by.
I tell you ___ to en - joy life, ___ I wish ___ I could ___ but it's too late.

Bridge

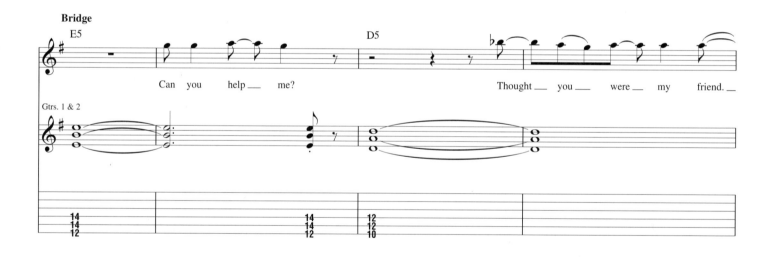

Can you help ___ me?

Thought ___ you ___ were ___ my friend. ___

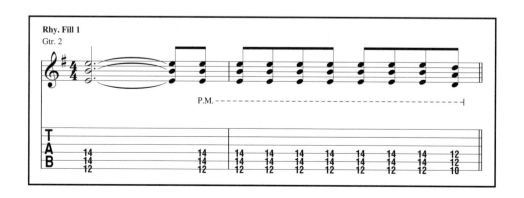

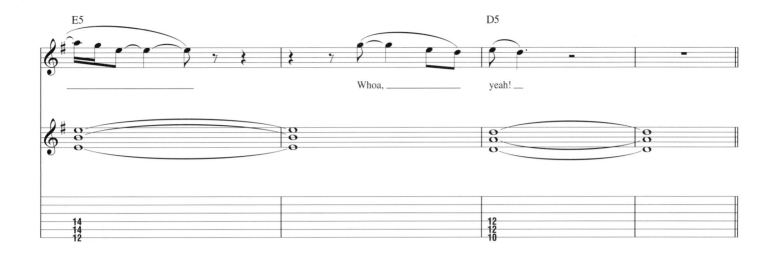

Whoa, _____ yeah! _____

Interlude

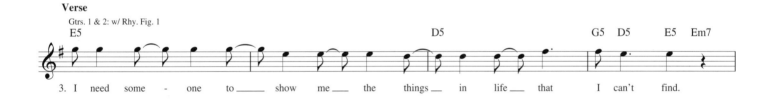

slight P.M.

Verse

Gtrs. 1 & 2: w/ Rhy. Fig. 1

3. I need some - one to _____ show me _____ the things _____ in life _____ that I can't find.

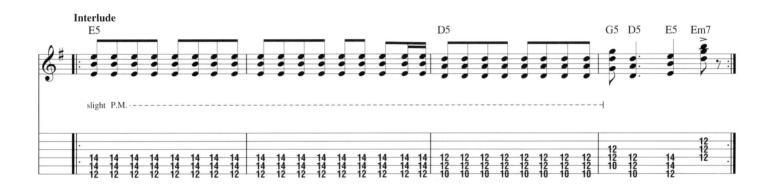

I can't see _____ the things _____ that make _____ true hap - pi - ness, _____ I must be blind.

Guitar solo

Gtr. 2: w/ Rhy. Fig. 1, 1st 4 meas., 4 times

*Gtr. 1

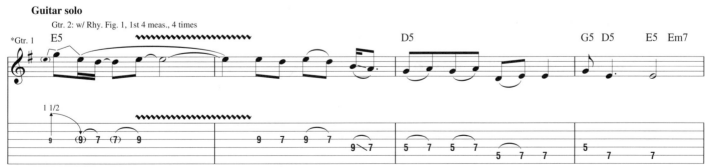

1 1/2

*With heavily distorted ring modulation effect in right channel.

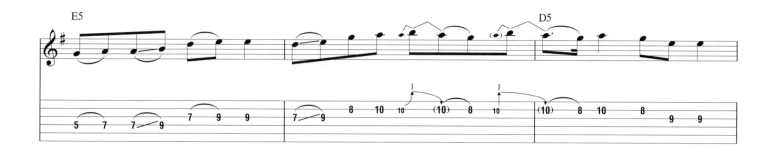

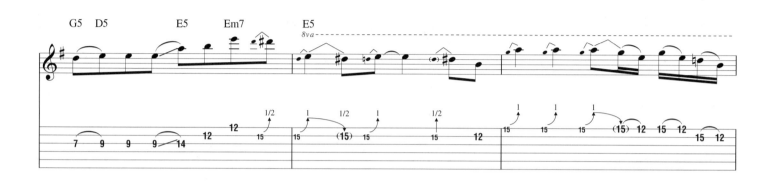

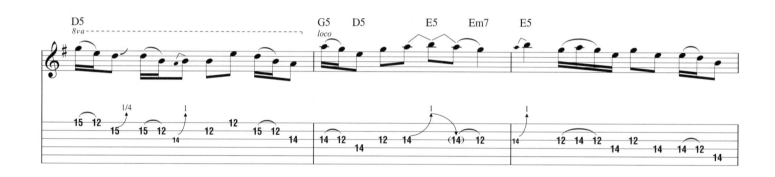

D.S. al Coda

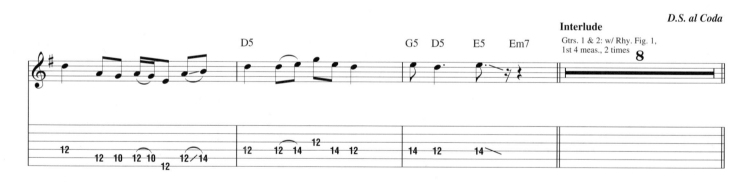

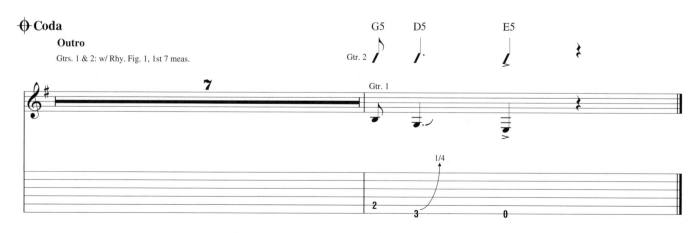

Pride and Joy

Written by Stevie Ray Vaughan

Verse

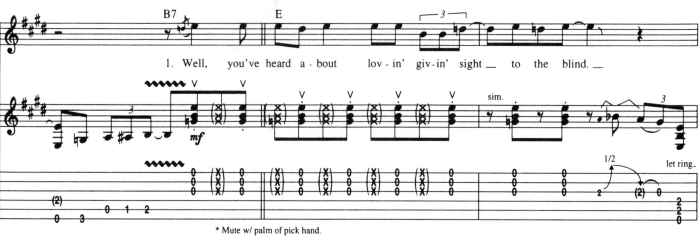

1. Well, you've heard a - bout lov-in' giv-in' sight __ to the blind. __

* Mute w/ palm of pick hand.

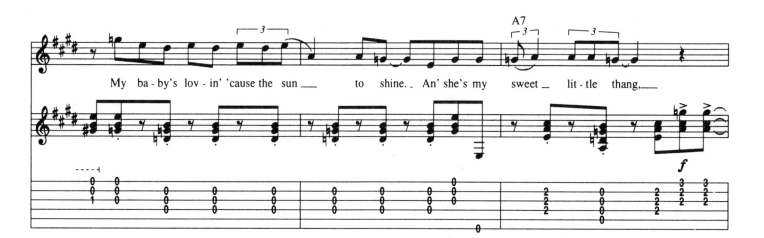

My ba - by's lov - in' 'cause the sun __ to shine. __ An' she's my sweet __ lit - tle thang, __

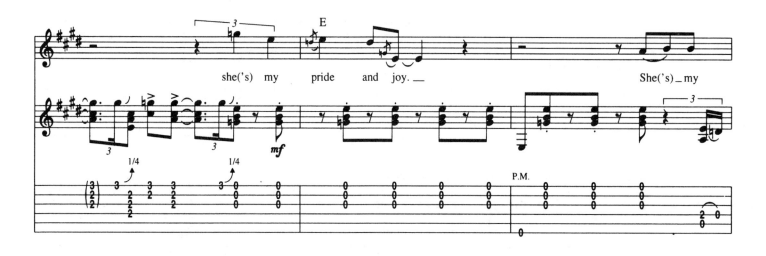

she('s) my pride and joy. __ She('s) __ my

sweet lit - tle ba - by, I'm __ her __ lit - tle lov - er boy. __

3. Yeah, I love my la-dy to be long and __ lean. __

You mess with her, you'll see a man get-tin' mean. __ She('s) my sweet __ lit-tle thang, __

she('s) my pride and joy. __ She('s) my

sweet _ lit-tle ba - by, I'm ____ her ____ lit - tle lov - er boy.

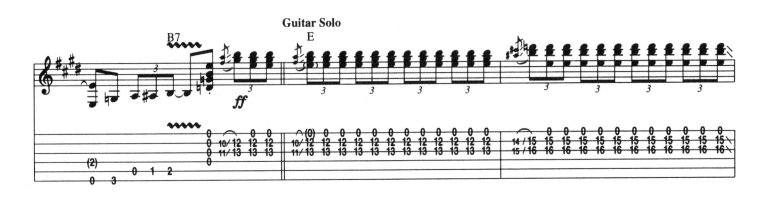

Guitar Solo

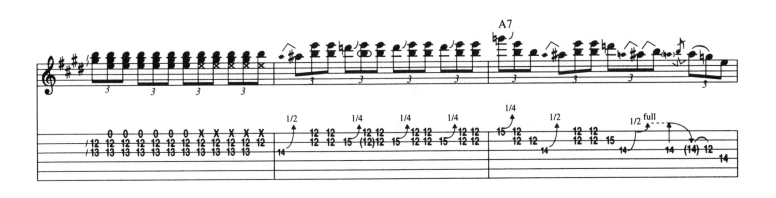

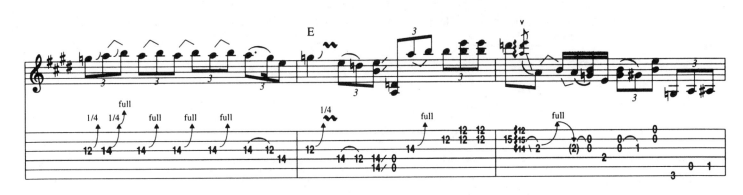

Verse

4. Well, I love my ba-by like the fin-est w, wine. _

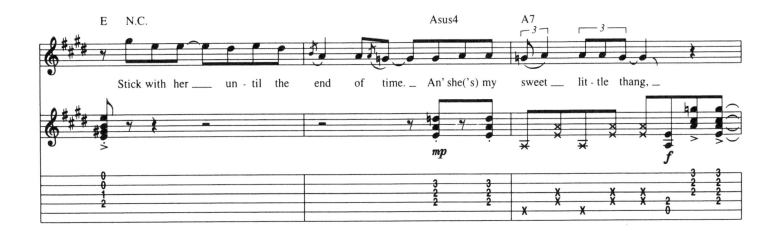

Stick with her ___ un-til the end of time. ___ An' she('s) my sweet ___ lit-tle thang, ___

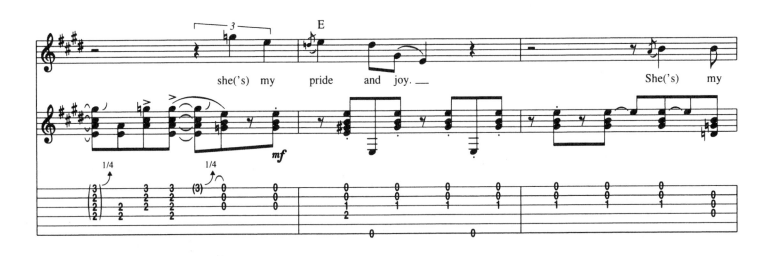

she('s) my pride and joy. ___ She('s) my

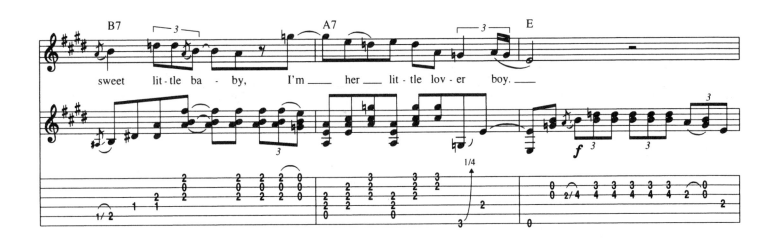

sweet lit-tle ba-by, I'm ___ her ___ lit-tle lov-er boy. ___

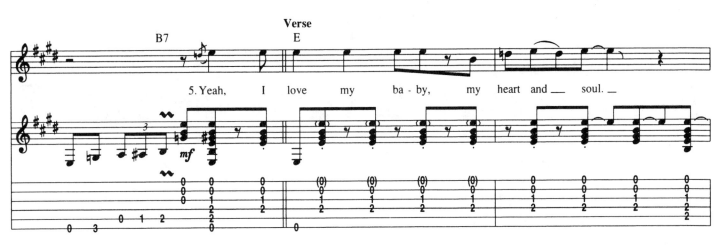

Verse

5. Yeah, I love my ba-by, my heart and ___ soul. ___

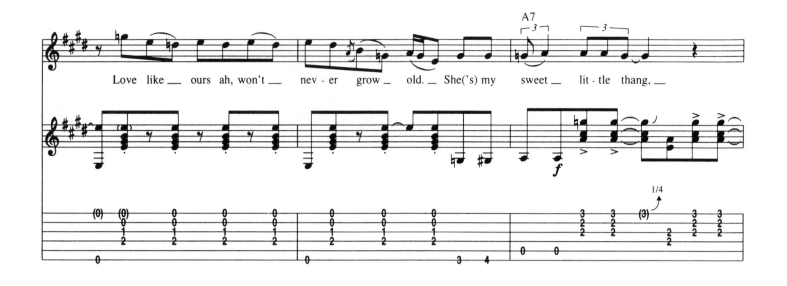

Love like — ours ah, won't — nev-er grow — old. — She('s) my — sweet — lit-tle thang, —

she('s) my pride and joy. — She('s) — my

sweet lit-tle ba-by, I'm — her — lit-tle lov-er boy. —

Guitar Solo

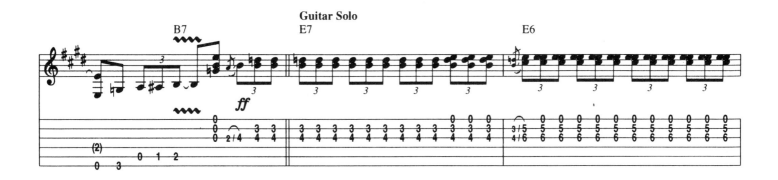

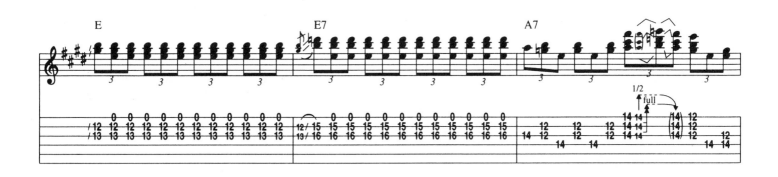

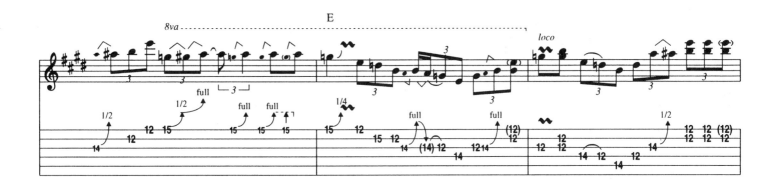

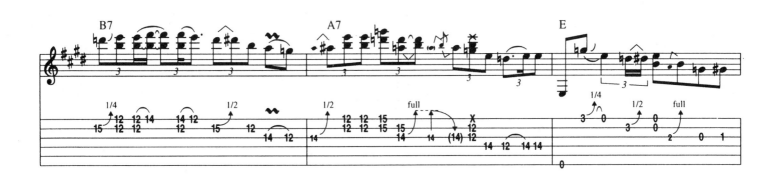

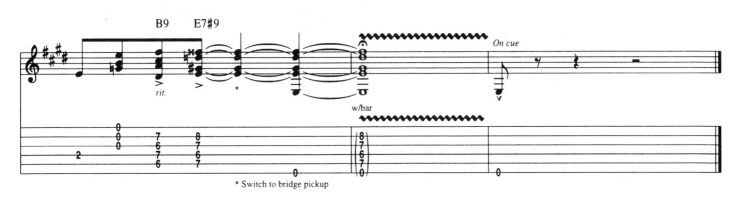

* Switch to bridge pickup

Raining Blood

Words and Music by Jeff Hanneman and Kerry King

Tune down 1/2 step:
(low to high) E♭-A♭-D♭-G♭-B♭-E♭

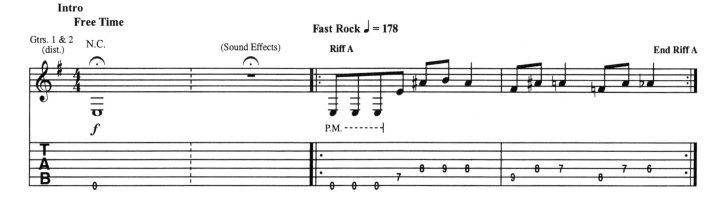

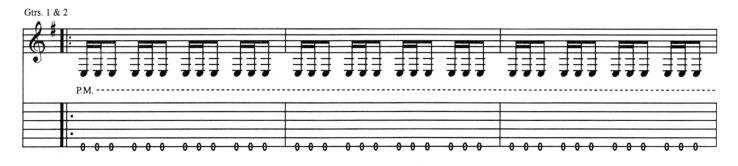

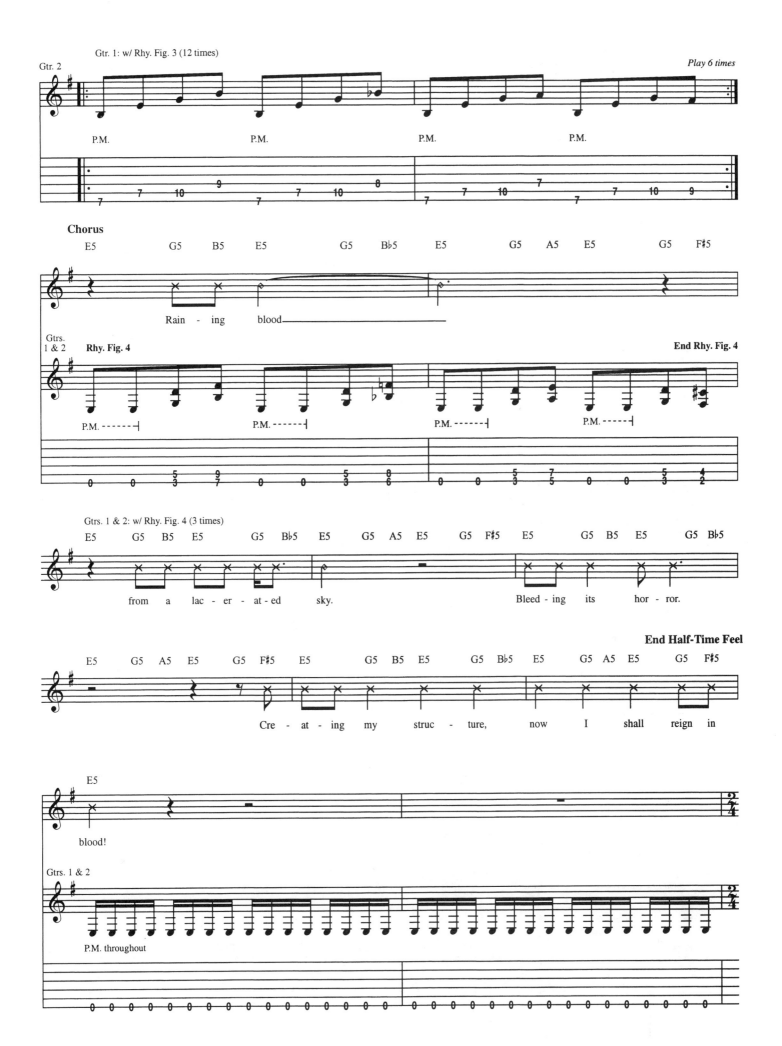

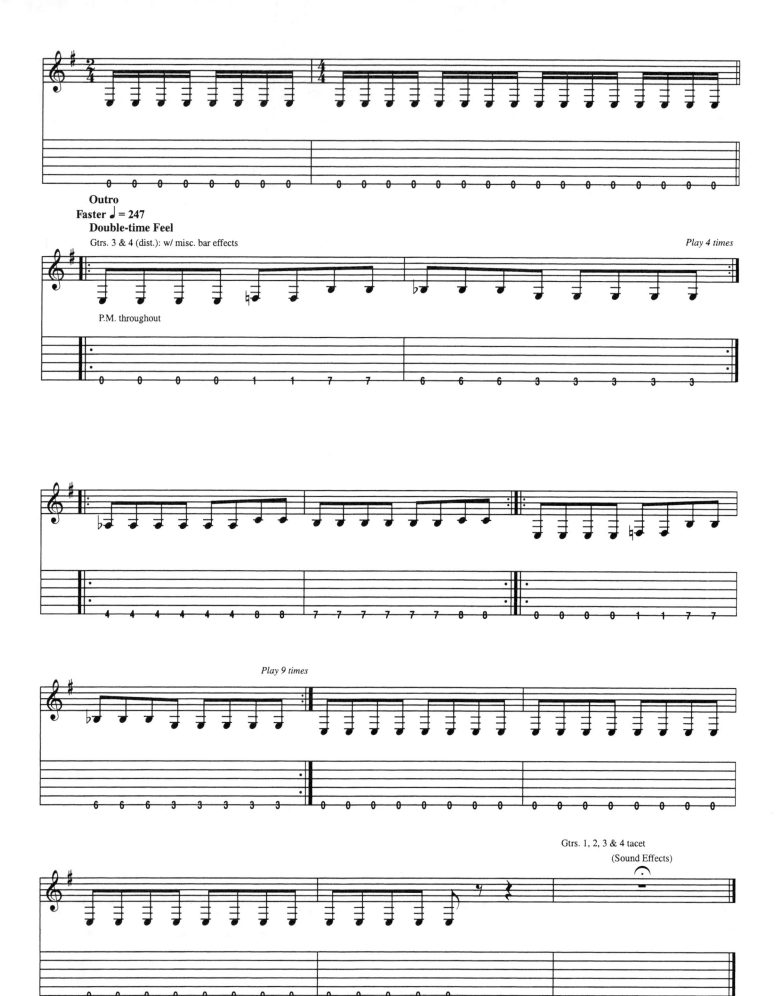

Outro
Faster ♩ = 247
Double-time Feel

Gtrs. 3 & 4 (dist.): w/ misc. bar effects

Play 4 times

P.M. throughout

Play 9 times

Gtrs. 1, 2, 3 & 4 tacet

(Sound Effects)

Rock and Roll All Nite

Words and Music by Paul Stanley and Gene Simmons

Tune Down 1/2 Step

①= Eb ④= Db

②= Bb ⑤= Ab

③= Gb ⑥= Eb

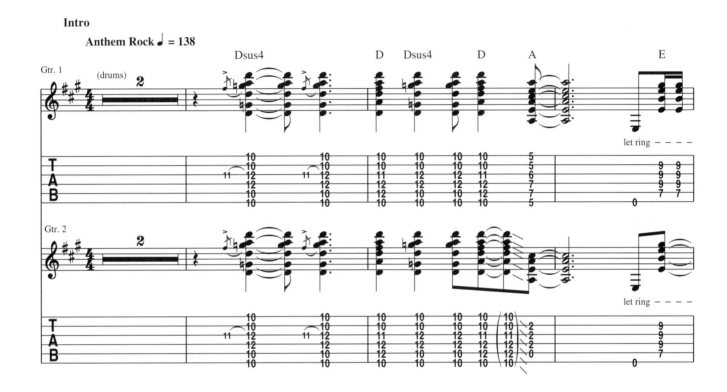

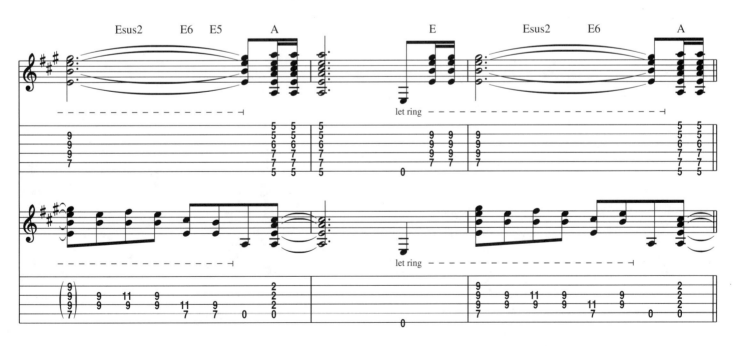

Verse

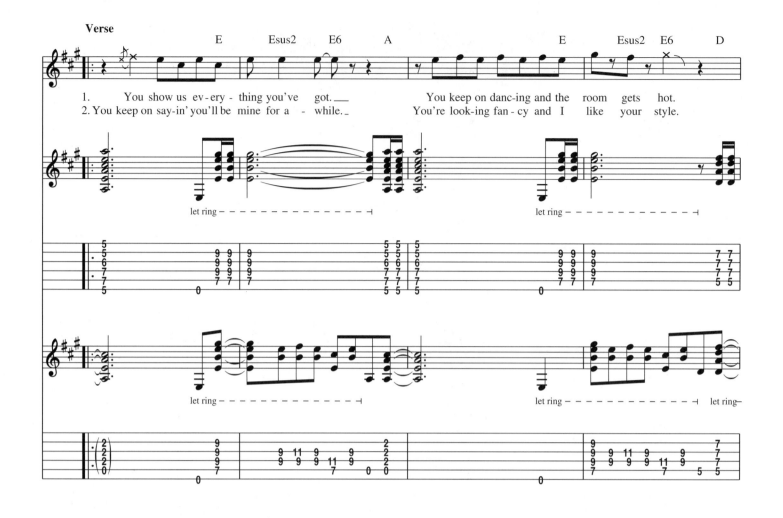

1. You show us ev-ery-thing you've got. __ You keep on danc-ing and the room gets hot.
2. You keep on say-in' you'll be mine for a - while. __ You're look-ing fan-cy and I like your style.

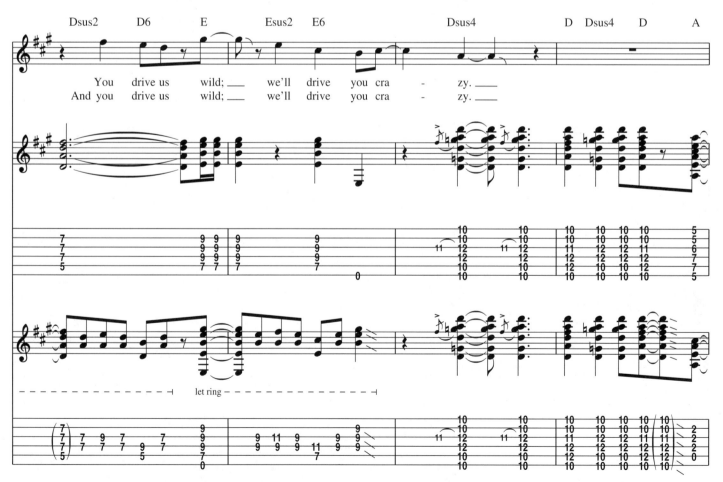

You drive us wild; __ we'll drive you cra - zy. __
And you drive us wild; __ we'll drive you cra - zy. __

And you say you wan-na go for a spin. __ The par-ty's just be-gun; we'll let you in.
And you show us ev-er-y-thing you've got. __ Oh ba-by, ba-by, that's quite a-lot.

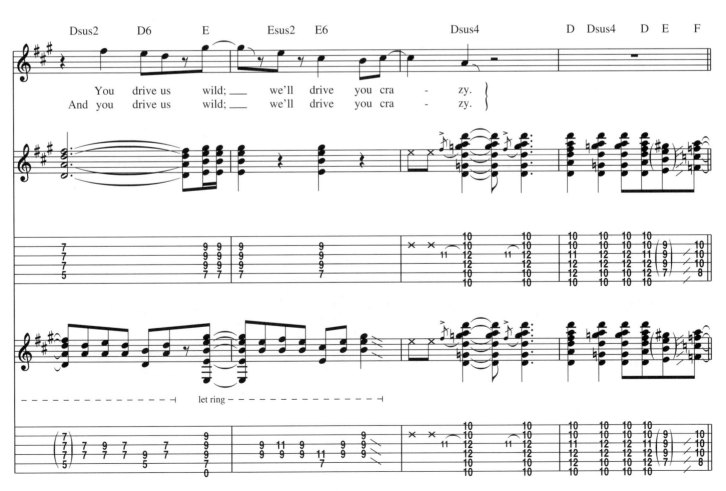

You drive us wild; __ we'll drive you cra-zy.
And you drive us wild; __ we'll drive you cra-zy.

Pre-Chorus

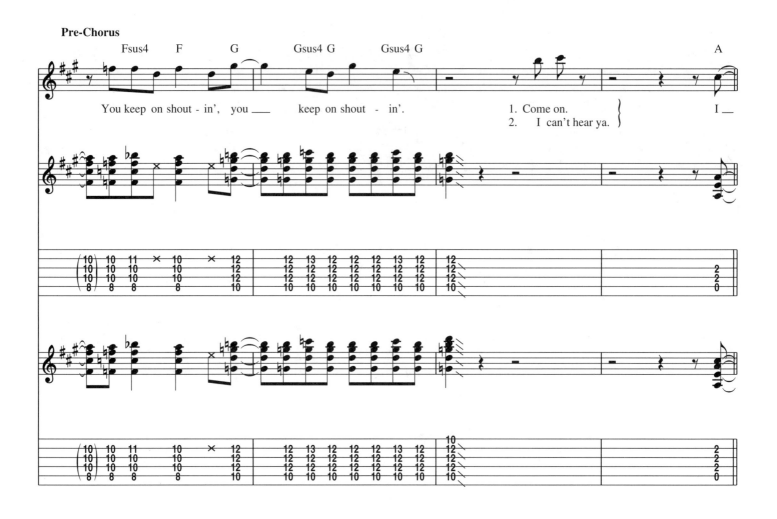

You keep on shout - in', you ___ keep on shout - in'. 1. Come on. 2. I can't hear ya. I ___

Chorus

___ wan - na rock and roll ___ all night, _____ and par - ty ev - ery day.

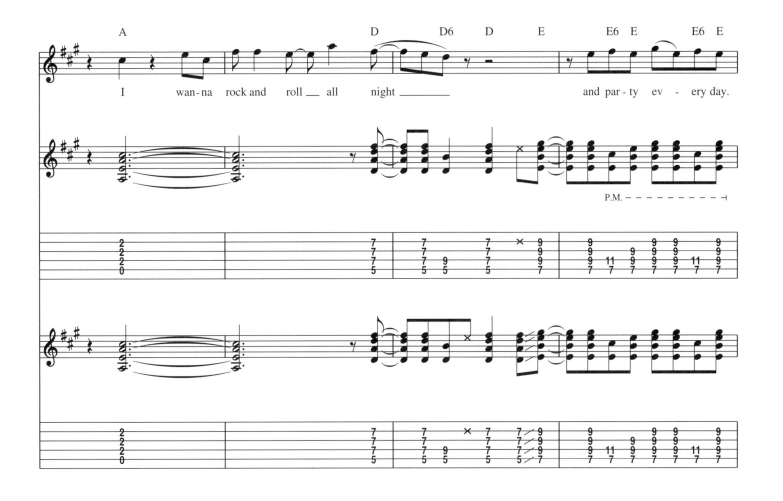

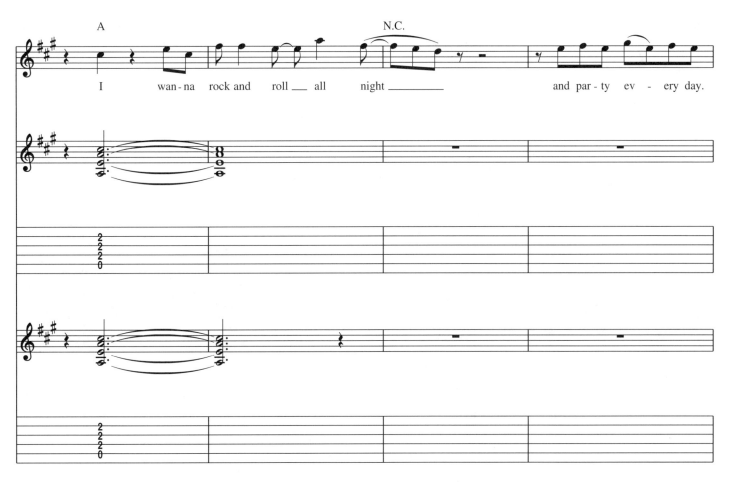

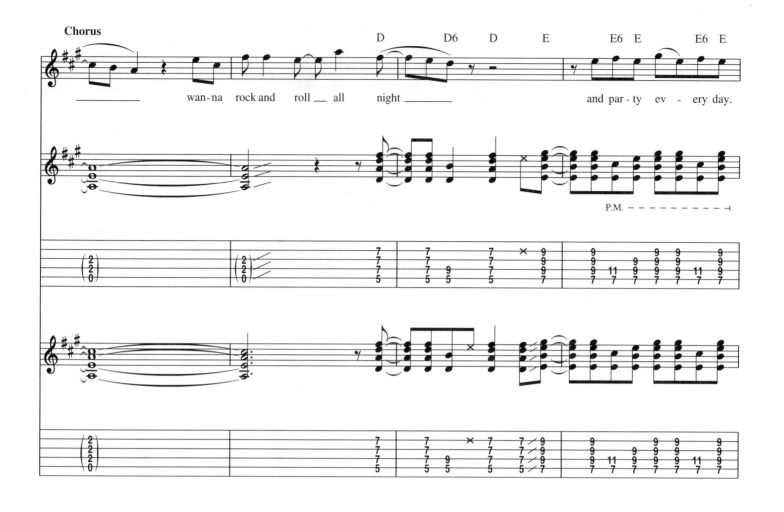

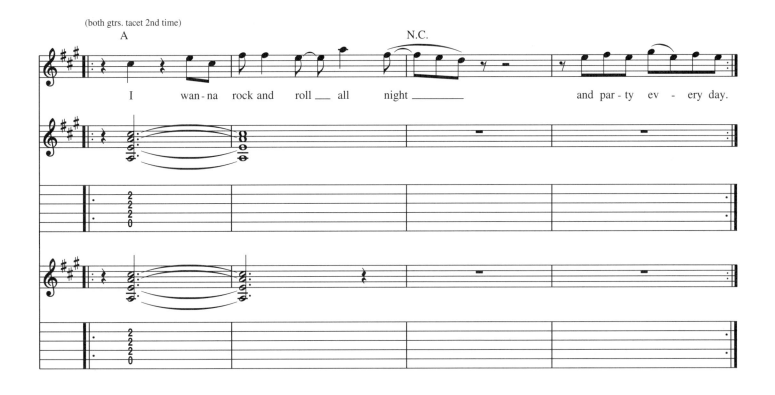

(both gtrs. tacet 2nd time)

I wan-na rock and roll __ all night _____ and par-ty ev - ery day.

Outro

Rock You Like a Hurricane

Words and Music by Herman Rarebell, Klaus Meine and Rudolf Schenker

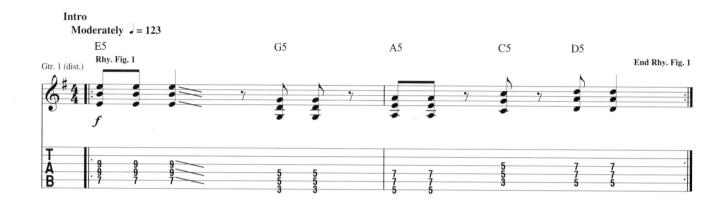

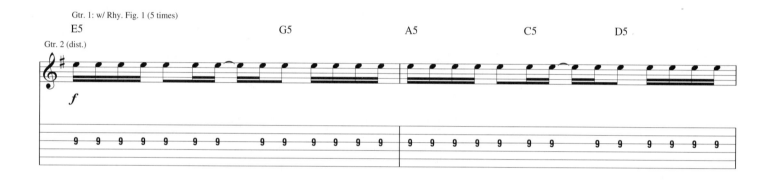

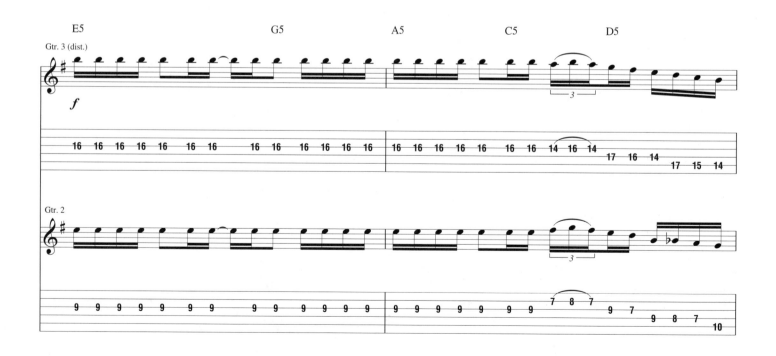

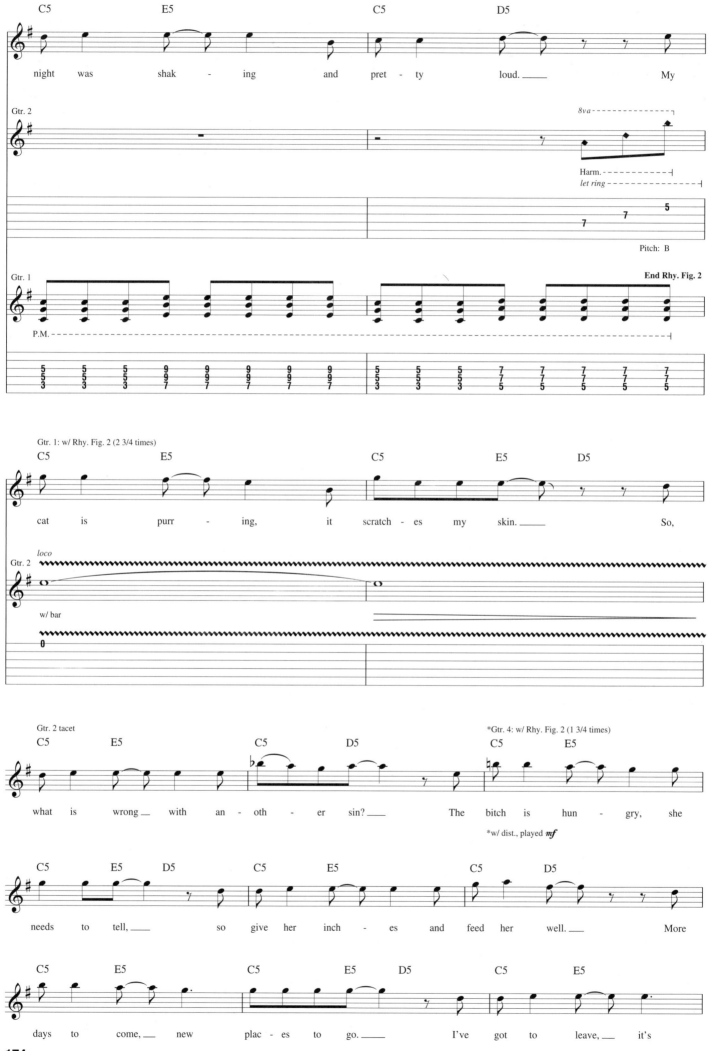

174

Guitar Solo

Gtr. 1: w/ Rhy. Fig. 1 (7 times)
Gtrs. 3 & 4 tacet

178

Coda

Outro-Chorus

*** As before

Pitch: B

Sabotage

Words and Music by Michael Diamond, Adam Yauch and Adam Horovitz

*Bass arr. for gtr.

**See top of page for chord diagram pertaining to rhythm slashes.

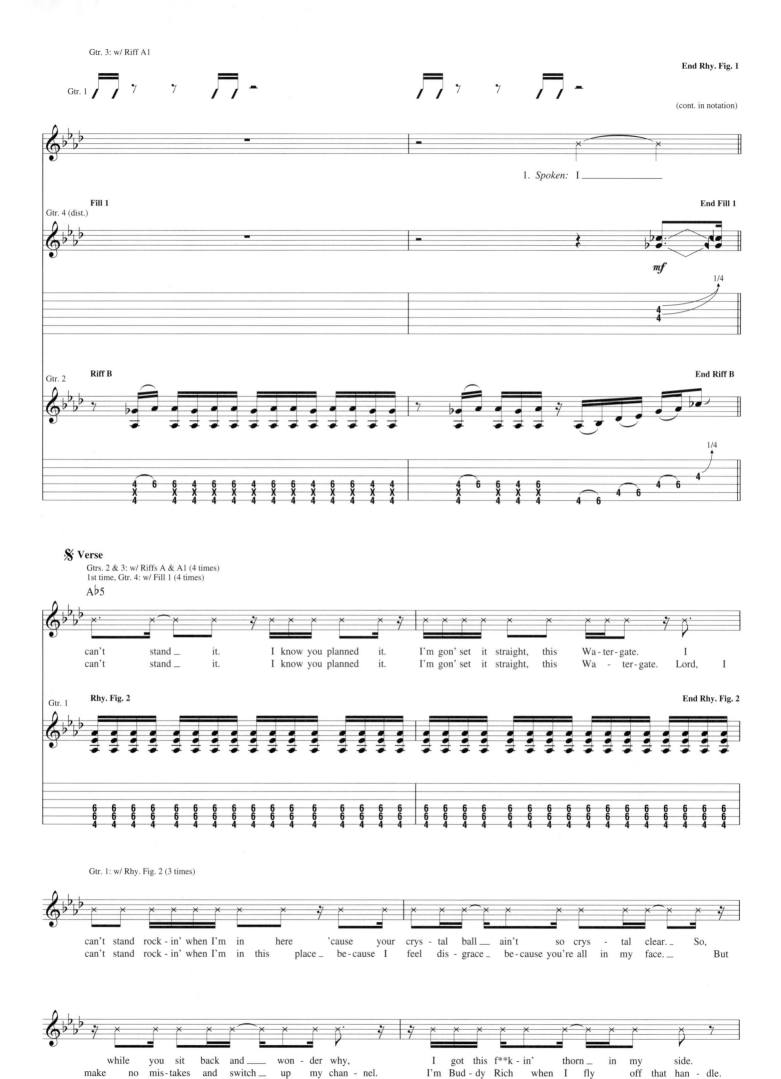

Oh, my God, it's a mi-rage. I'm tell-in' y'all it's sab - o - tage.
What could it be? It's a mi-rage. You're schem-in' on a thing that's sab - o - tage.

Turntable Solo

Gtr. 1: w/ Rhy. Fig. 1
Gtr. 2: w/ Riff A   Gtr. 2: w/ Riff B
Gtr. 3: w/ Riff A1 (2 times)

A♭5   N.C.

2

2. So, so, so,

Fill 2   End Fill 2
Gtr. 4

Verse

Gtr. 1: w/ Rhy. Fig. 2 (2 times)
Gtrs. 2 & 3: w/ Riffs A & A1 (2 times)
Gtr. 4 tacet

A♭5

so lis - ten up 'cause you can't say noth - in'. You shut me down with a push of your but - ton. But you,

I'm out and ___ I'm gone. I'll tell you now, I keep ___ it on ___ and on.

Gtr. 4

Guitar Solo

Gtr. 4 tacet
N.C.

Gtr. 1

f

183

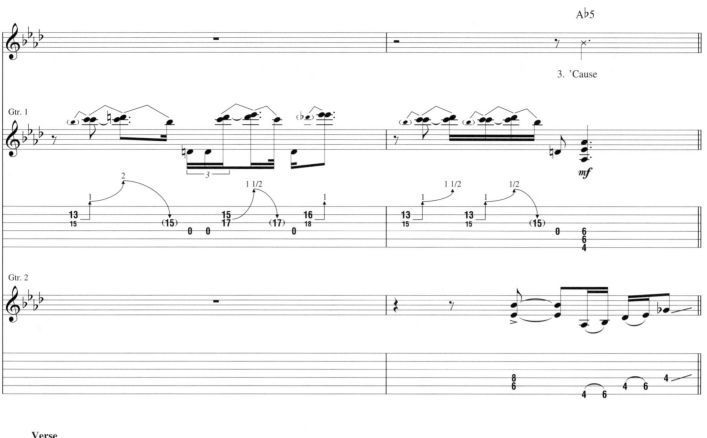

Ab5

3. 'Cause

mf

Verse
Gtr. 1: w/ Rhy. Fig. 2 (2 times)
Gtrs. 2 & 3: w/ Riffs A & A1 (2 times)

Ab5

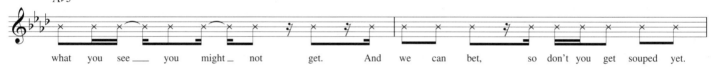

what you see___ you might___ not get. And we can bet, so don't you get souped yet.

Gtr. 4: w/ Fill 2

Schem-in' on a thing that's a mi-rage.___ I'm try-in' to tell you now it's sab - o - tage.___

Turntable Solo
Gtr. 1: w/ Rhy. Fig. 1   Gtr. 3 tacet
Gtrs. 2 & 3: w/ Riffs A & A1 (1 1/2 times)

Ab5   N.C.

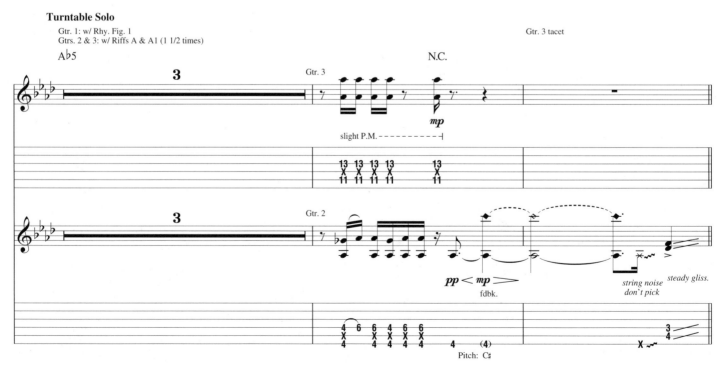

slight P.M.

mp

pp < mp >
fdbk.

string noise
don't pick

steady gliss.

Pitch: C#

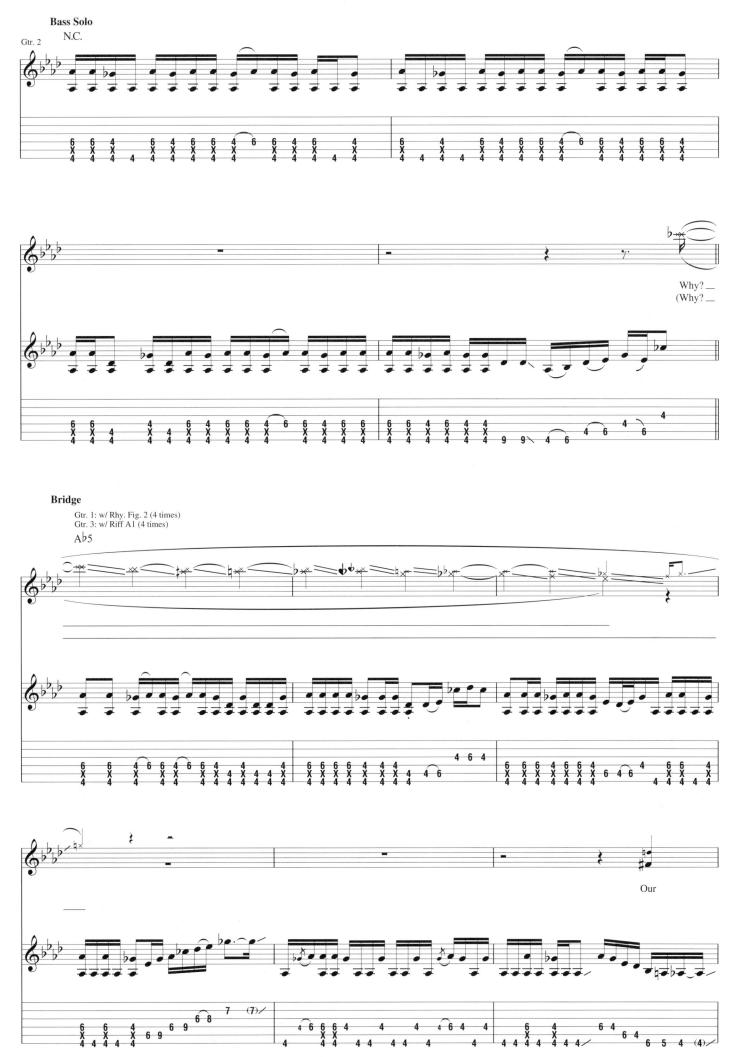

Same Old Song and Dance

Words and Music by Steven Tyler and Joe Perry

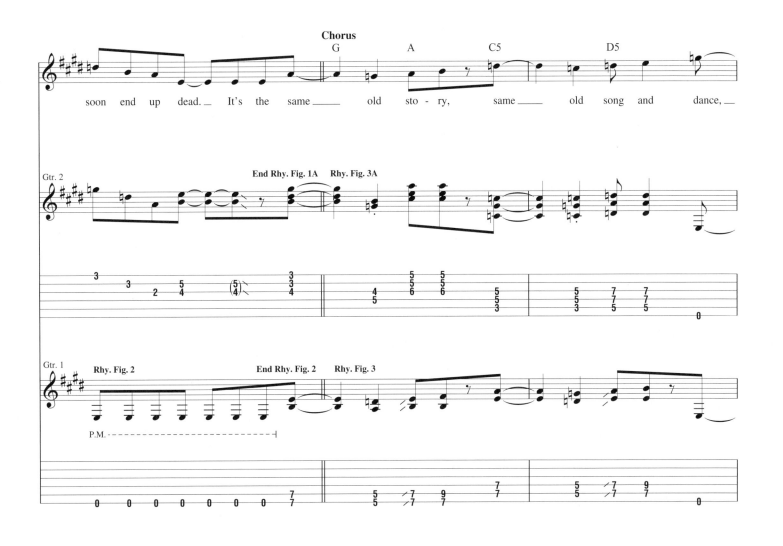

soon end up dead.   It's the same ___ old sto - ry,   same ___ old song and   dance, ___

my friend. ___   It's the same ___ old sto - ry,   same ___

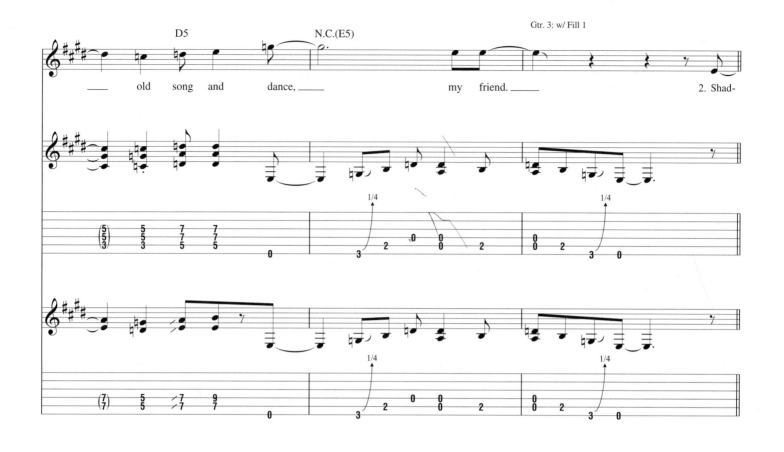

old song and dance, _____ my friend. _____ 2. Shad-

𝄋 Verse

Gtr. 1: w/ Rhy. Fig. 1, 3 times
Gtr. 2: w/ Rhy. Fig. 1A

N.C.(E5)

-y look-in' los-er you played with my gun. _____ No smooth _____ face law-yer can
_____ down and dirt-y from walk-in' the street _____ with your old _____ hur-dy, gur-dy,

Gtr. 1: w/ Rhy. Fig. 1, 2 times

get you un-done. _____ } Say love _____ ain't the same on the south side o' town. _____ You could look_
no one to meet. _____ }

but you ain't gon-na find it a - round. It's the same ___ old sto - ry, same __

__ old song and dance, ___ my friend. ___ It's the same __

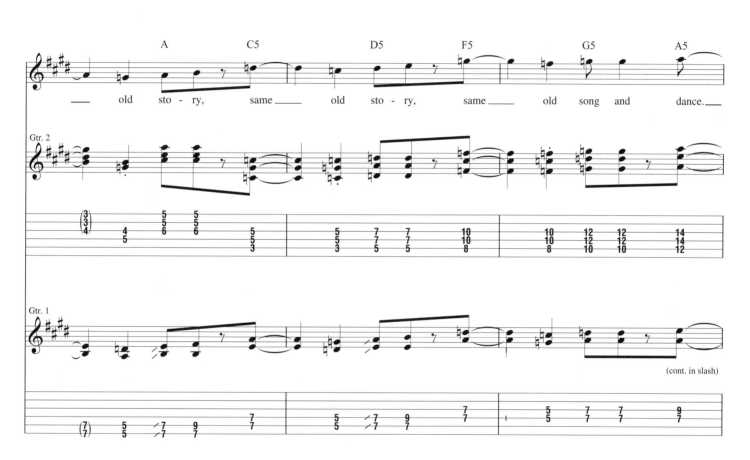

__ old sto - ry, same ___ old sto - ry, same ___ old song and dance. __

(cont. in slash)

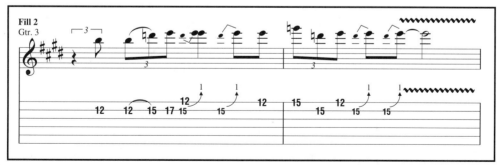

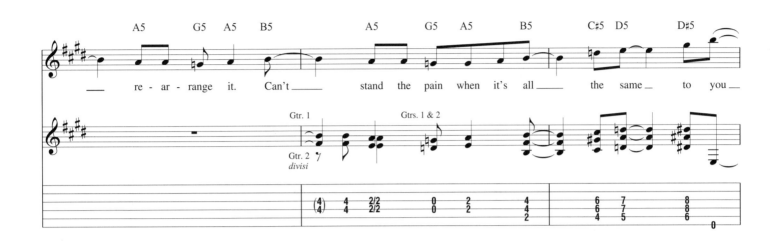

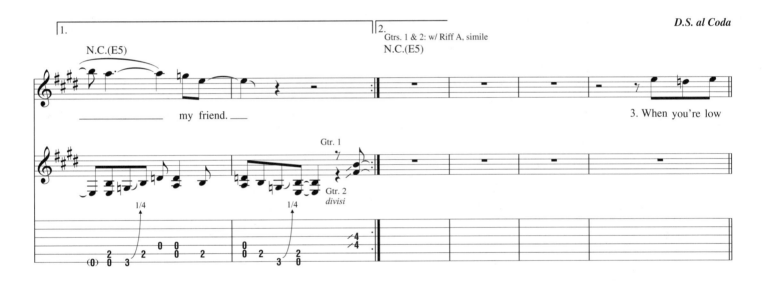

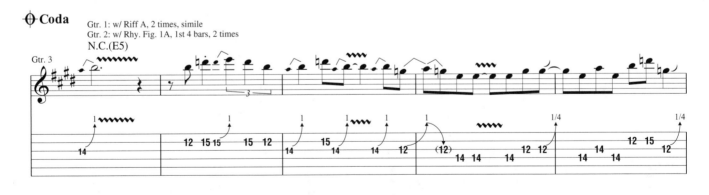

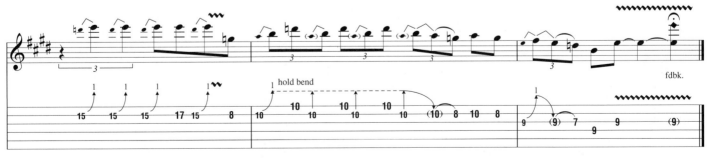

School's Out

Words and Music by Alice Cooper and Michael Bruce

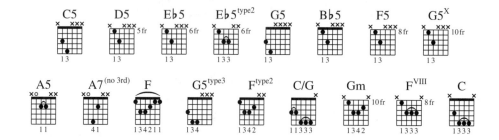

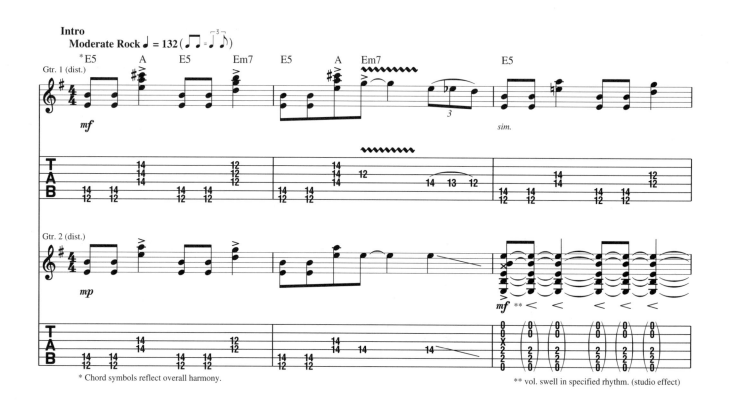

* Chord symbols reflect overall harmony.

** vol. swell in specified rhythm. (studio effect)

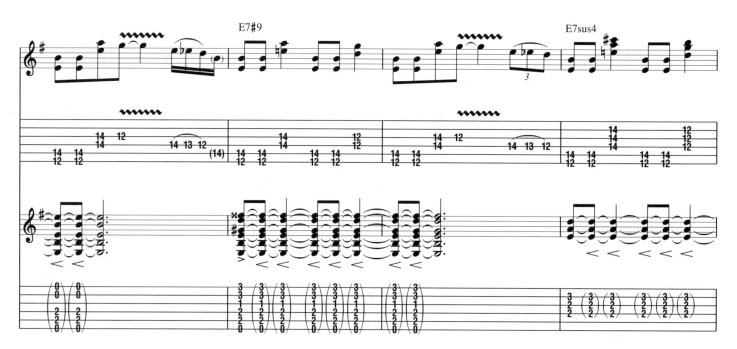

Pre-Chorus

can't sa- lute ___ ya, can't find a flag. ___ If that don't suit ya, that's a drag. ___

Chorus

School's out for sum-mer!

196

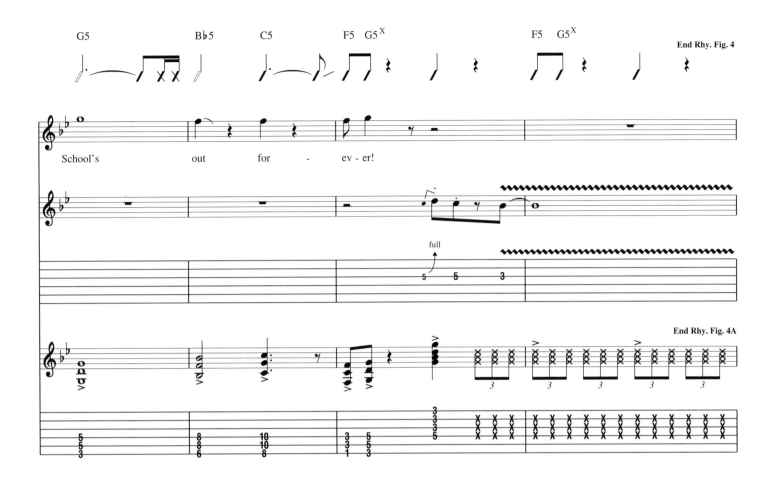

School's   out   for   ev - er!

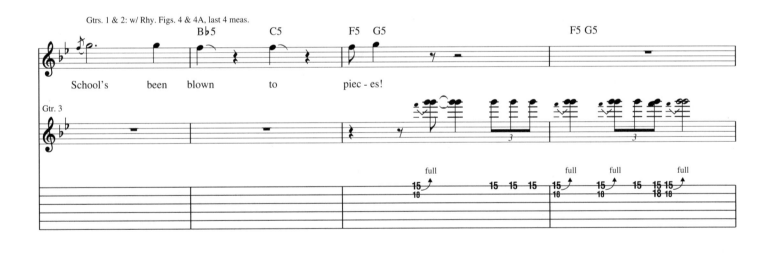

School's   been   blown   to   piec - es!

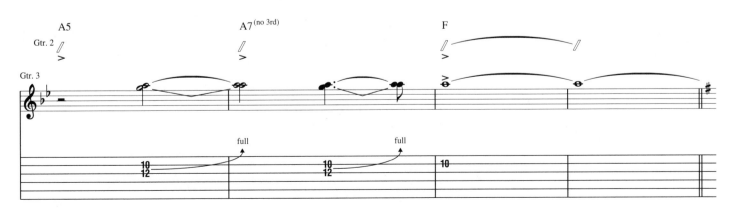

Bridge

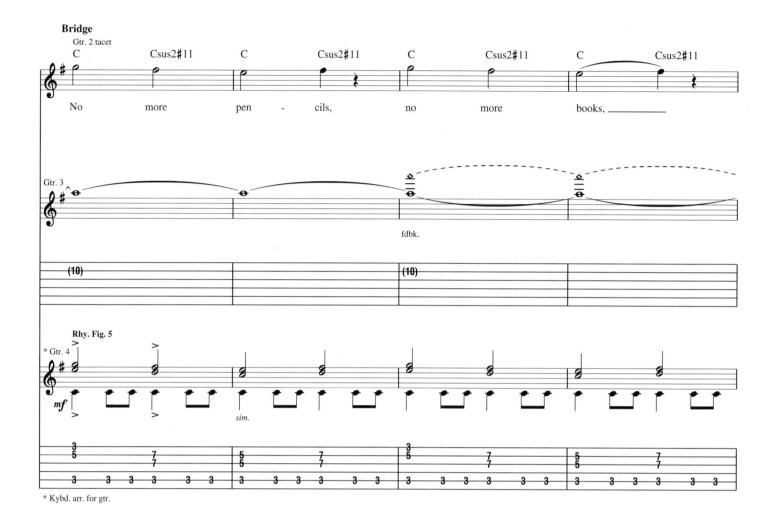

No more pen - cils, no more books,

* Kybd. arr. for gtr.

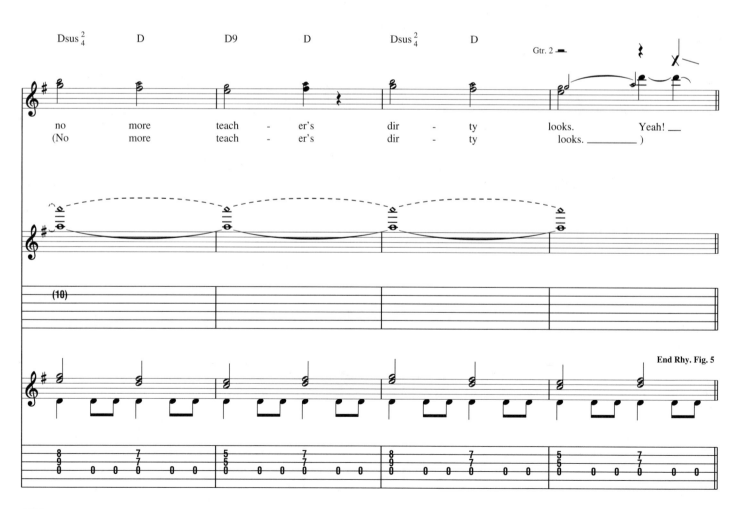

no more teach - er's dir - ty looks. Yeah!
(No more teach - er's dir - ty looks.)

The Seeker

Words and Music by Pete Townshend

Slow Ride

Words and Music by David Peverett

Gtr. 2: Open E tuning:
(low to high) E-B-E-G♯-B-E

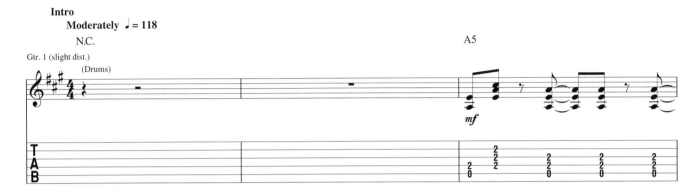

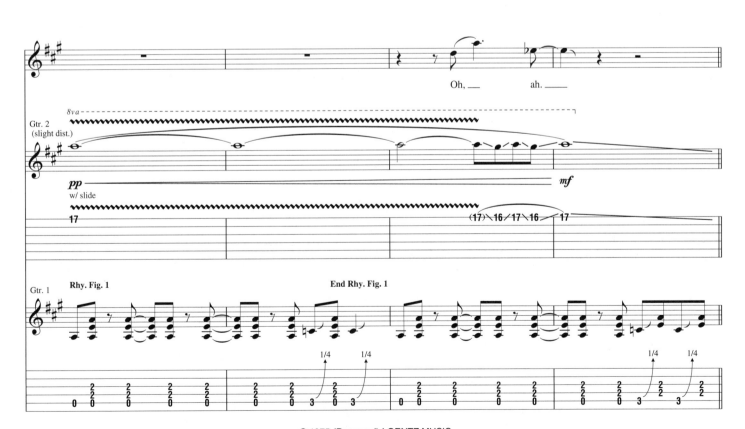

Verse

1. I'm in the mood. _____ The rhy - thm is right. _____

*Chord symbols reflect combined harmony.

Move to the mu - sic, we can

roll all night. ___   Oo, _____

slow ___ ride.

Oo. _____

Slow rid - in' wom - an, you're so ____ fine.

Interlude

N.C.

Woo!

let ring ----------|

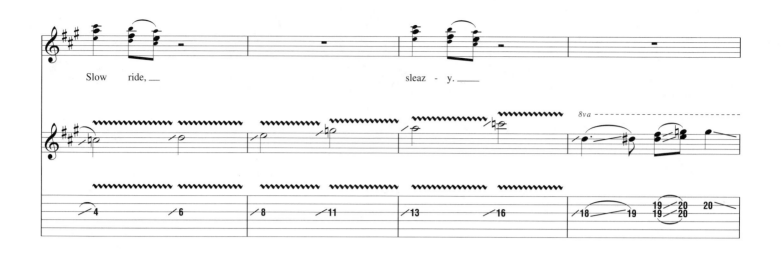

Slow ride, ___ sleaz - y. ___

Begin fade

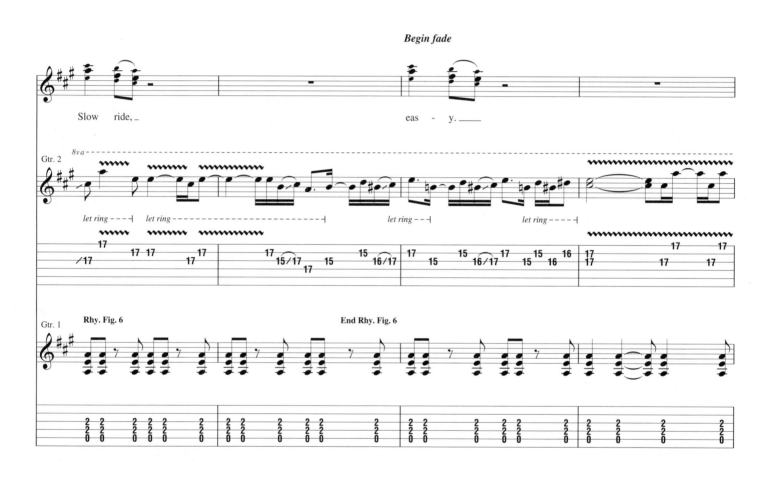

Slow ride, ___ eas - y. ___

Gtr. 2

let ring *let ring* *let ring* *let ring*

Gtr. 1   **Rhy. Fig. 6**   **End Rhy. Fig. 6**

Gtr. 1: w/ Rhy. Fig. 6 (till fade)   ***Fade out***

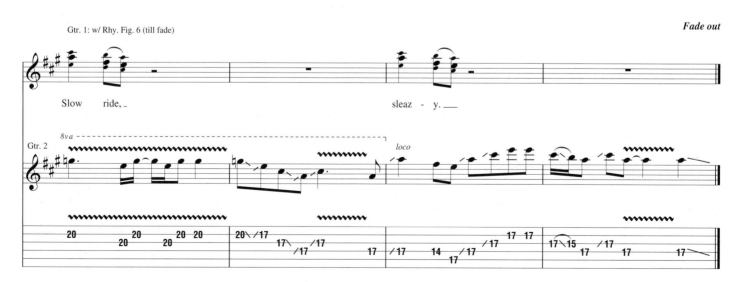

Slow ride, ___ sleaz - y. ___

Gtr. 2

loco

Story of My Life

Words and Music by Michael Ness

* Symbols in parentheses represent chord names respective to capoed guitars.
  Capoed fret is "0" in TAB.

215

Stricken

Words and Music by David Draiman, Dan Donegan and Mike Wengren

Drop D tuning, down 1 step:
(low to high) C-G-C-F-A-D

Intro
Moderately ♩ = 88

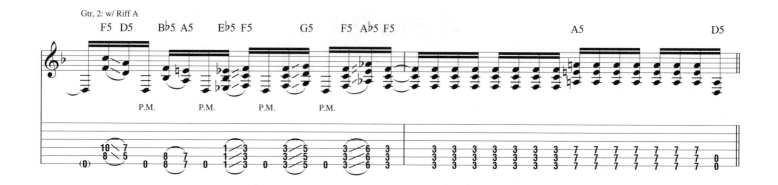

221

Verse

Gtr. 1: w/ Rhy. Fig. 1

D5   F5   G5   D5   F5   G5   D5   F5   D5

____ 2. You don't know what your pow-er has done to me.   I want to know if I'll heal ____ in - side.

Gtr. 2: w/ Riff A

F5   G5   F5   A5   D5

I can't go on with a hol-o-caust a-bout to hap - pen, see-ing you laugh - ing an-oth-er time.

*F5   G5   D5   F5   G5   D5   F5   D5

You'll nev - er know why your face has haunt-ed me.   My ver - y soul has to bleed this ___ time.

Gtr. 1   **Riff C**

*Chord symbols reflect implied harmony, next 3 meas.

D.S. al Coda

Gtr. 2: w/ Riff B

F5   G5   F5   A5

An-oth-er hole in the wall of my in - ner de-fens - es, leav-in' me breath - less. The rea - son I

End Riff C

Coda

Interlude

D5

run.

Rhy. Fig. 2   **End Rhy. Fig. 2**

Gtr. 1: w/ Rhy. Fig. 2

In - to _____ the _____ a - byss will _____ I _____

Guitar Solo

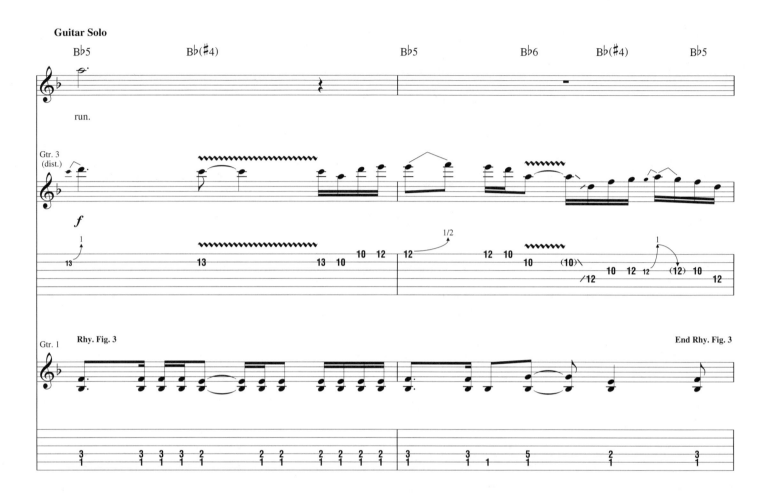

run.

Gtr. 3
(dist.)

f

Gtr. 1   Rhy. Fig. 3   End Rhy. Fig. 3

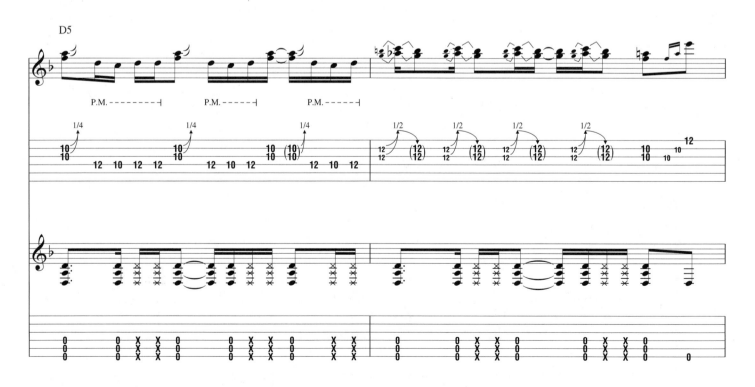

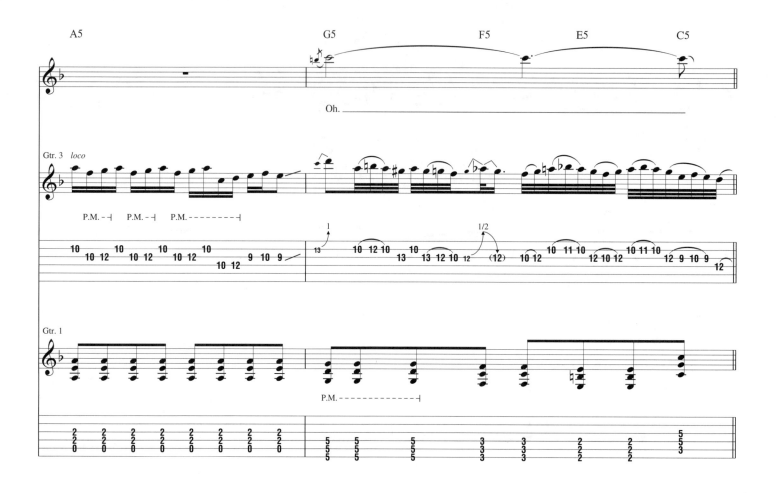

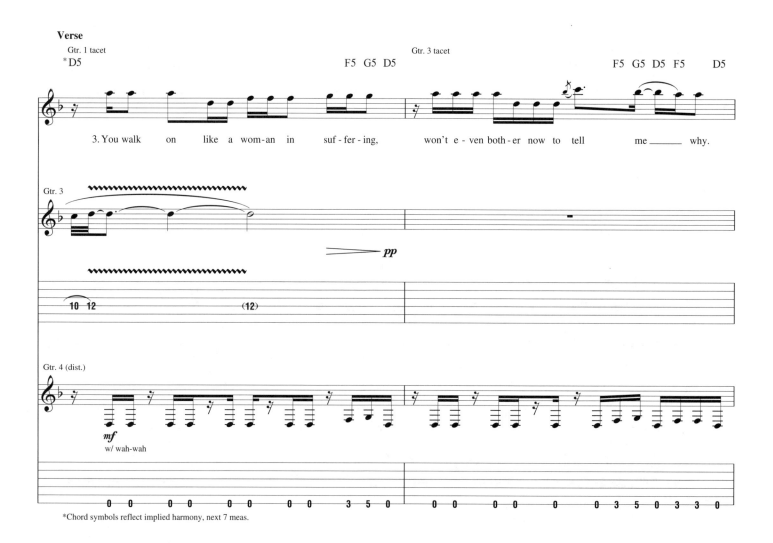

*Chord symbols reflect implied harmony, next 7 meas.

Gtr. 2: w/ Riff A

You come a-long, let-ting all of us sa-vor the mo - ment, leav-in' me bro - ken an-oth-er time.

Gtr. 4

Gtr. 5 (dist.)

Gtr. 1: w/ Riff C
Gtrs. 4 & 5 tacet

You come on like a blood stained hur-ri-cane. Leave me a-lone, let me be ___ this ___ time.

Gtr. 1: w/ Riff B

You car-ry on like a ho - ly man push-ing re-demp - tion. Don't wan-na mem - tion the rea-son I

Chorus

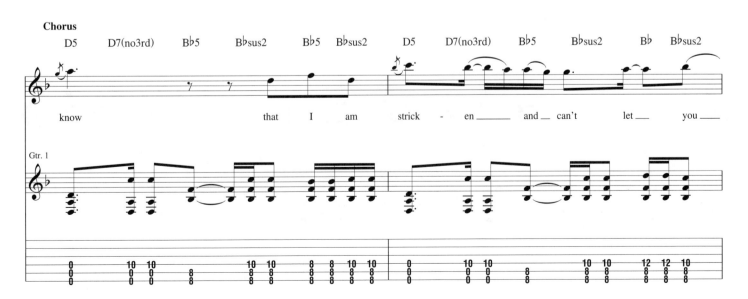

know that I am strick - en ___ and ___ can't let ___ you ___

Gtr. 1

227

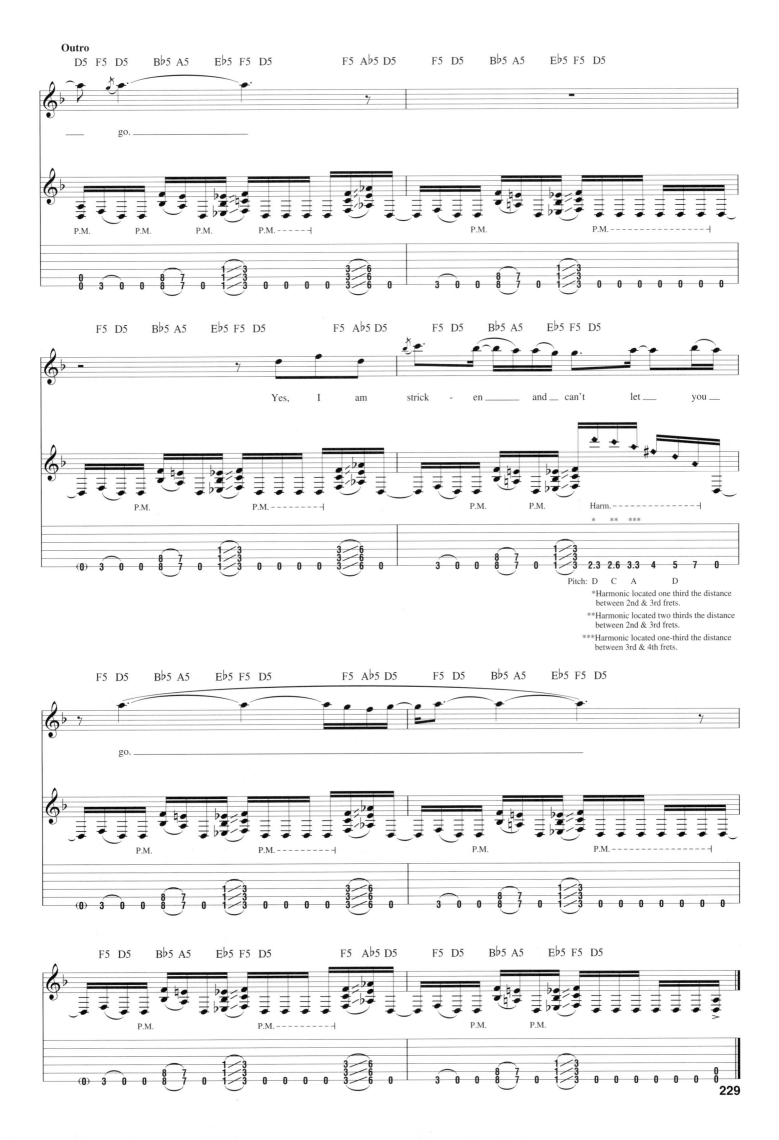

Suck My Kiss

Words and Music by Anthony Kiedis, Flea, John Frusciante and Chad Smith

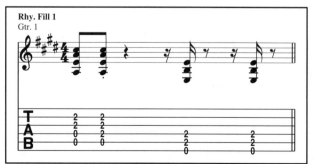

Give to me sweet sa-cred bliss, that mouth was made to suck my kiss!

Sunshine of Your Love

Words and Music by Jack Bruce, Pete Brown and Eric Clapton

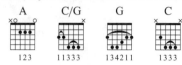

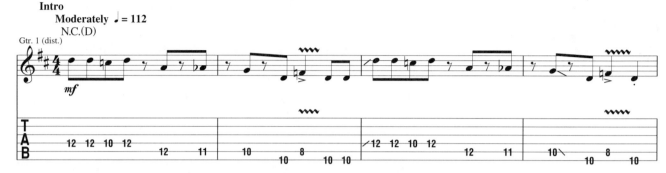

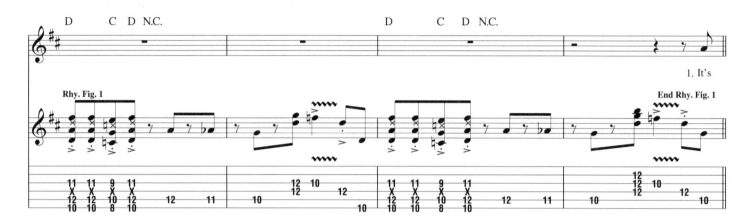

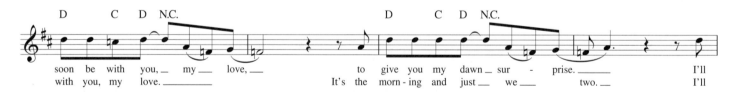

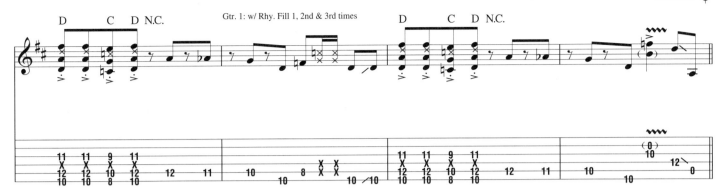

Chorus

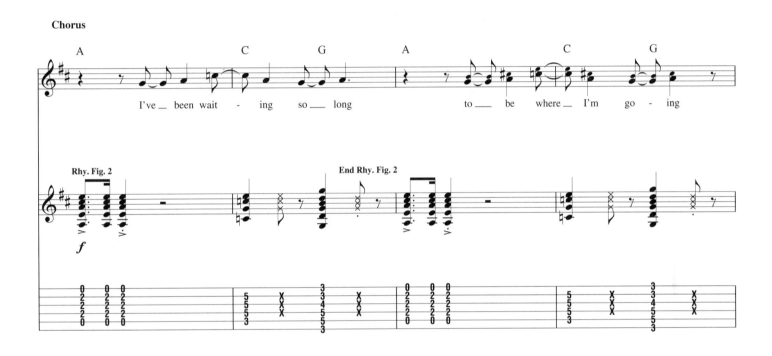

I've __ been wait - ing so __ long   to __ be where __ I'm go - ing

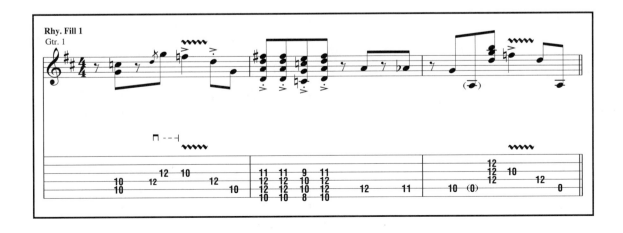

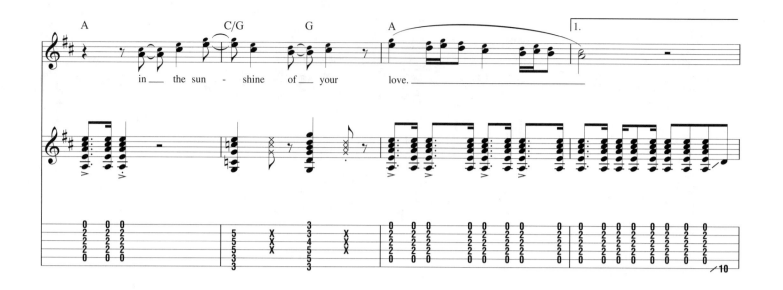

in __ the sun - shine of __ your love. ___

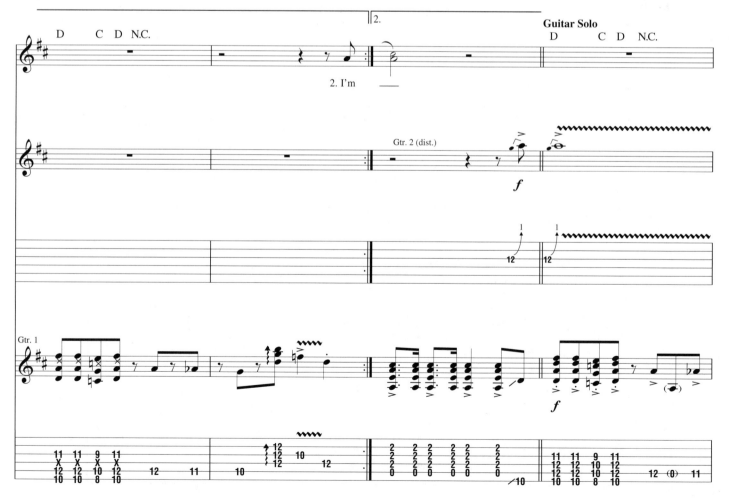

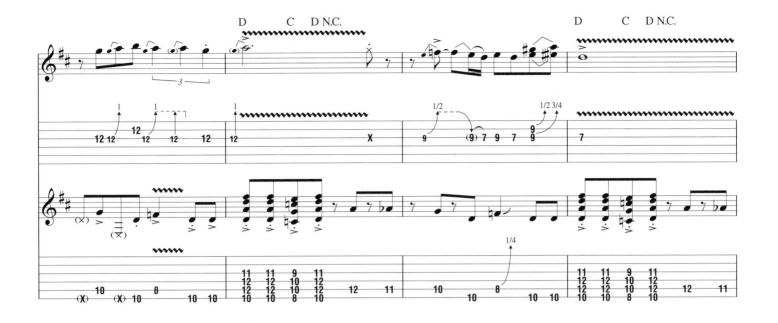

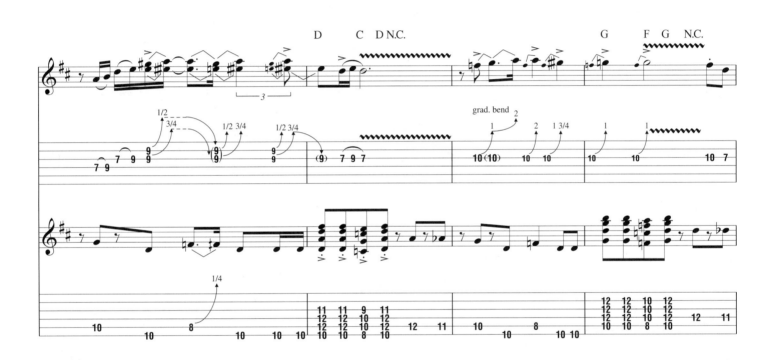

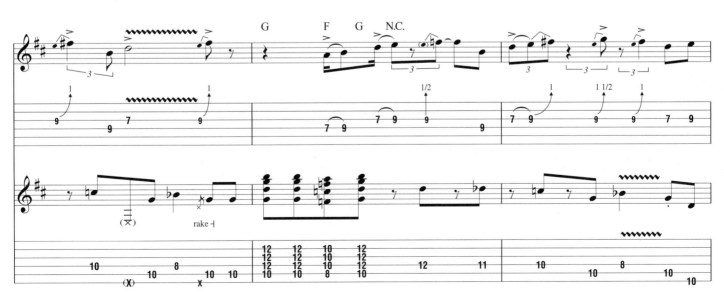

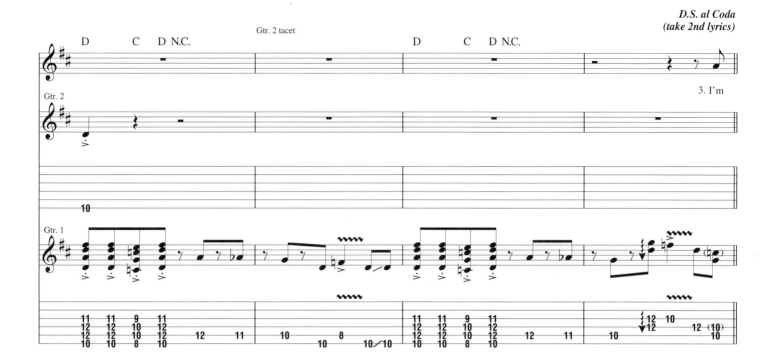

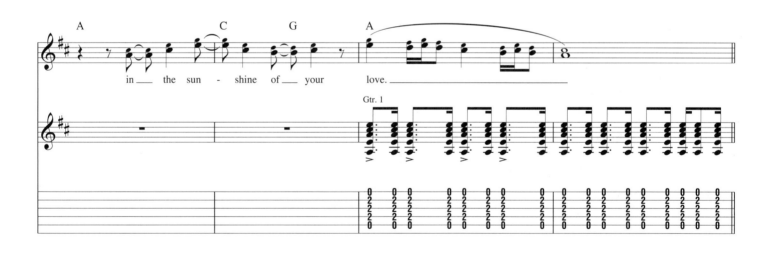

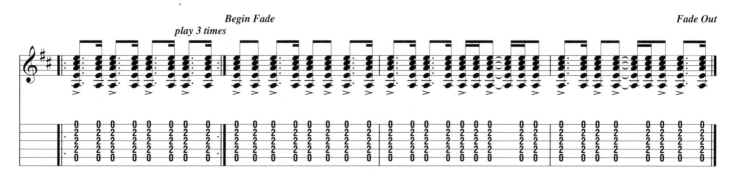

Talk Dirty to Me

Words and Music by Bobby Dall, Brett Michaels, Bruce Johannesson and Rikki Rockett

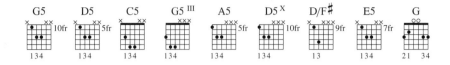

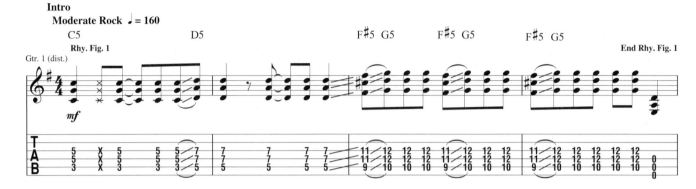

Tune down 1/2 step:
(low to high) Eb-Ab-Db-Gb-Bb-Eb

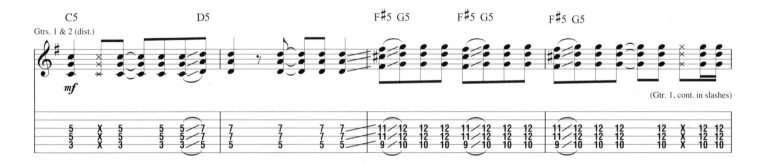

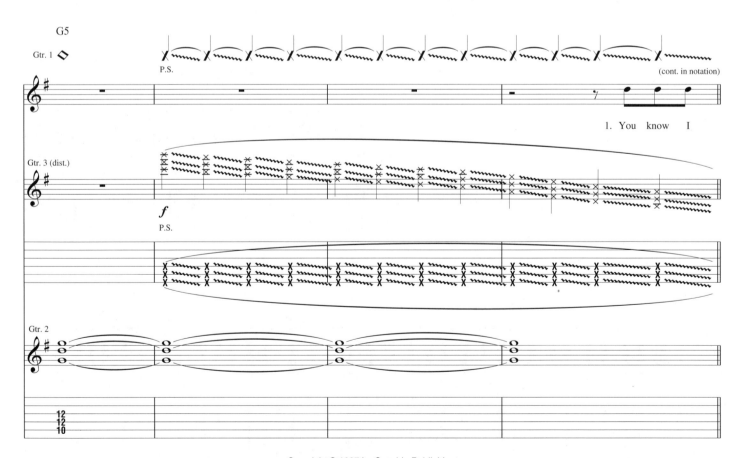

Verse

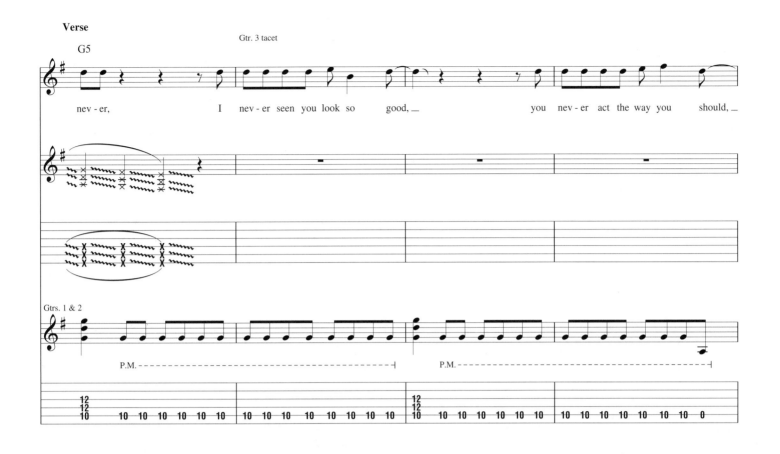

never, I nev-er seen you look so good, ___ you nev-er act the way you should, ___

___ uh, but I like ___ it. And I

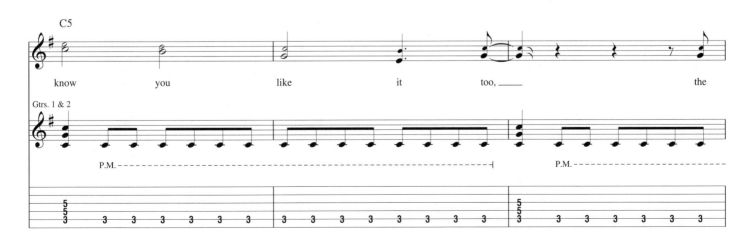

know you like it too, ___ the

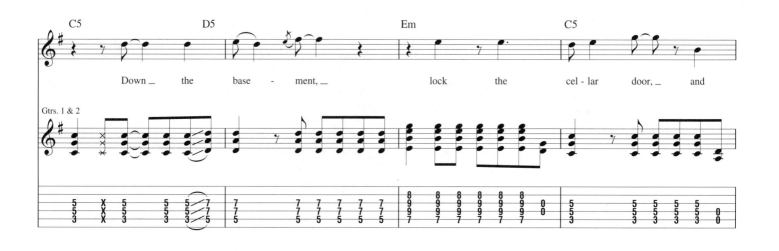

Down _ the base - ment, _ lock the cel - lar door, _ and

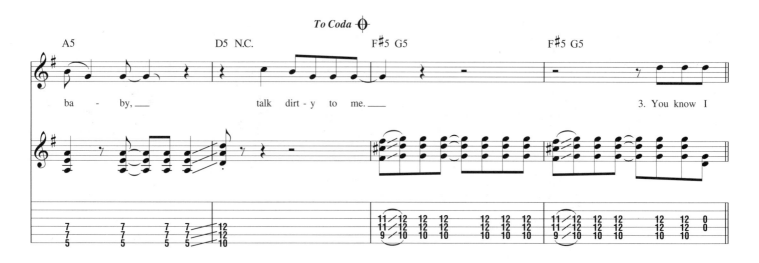

To Coda

ba - by, _ talk dirt - y to me. _ 3. You know I

Verse

call you, I call _ you on the tel - e - phone, _ I'm on - ly hop - in' that you're home _

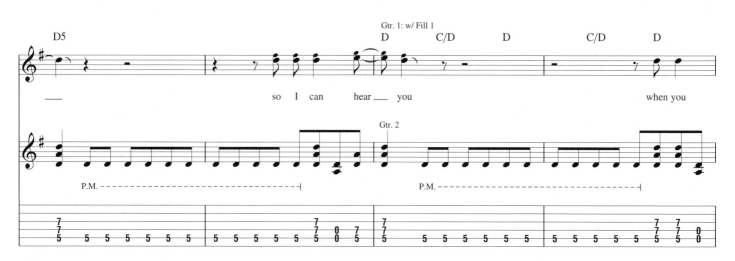

_ so I can hear _ you when you

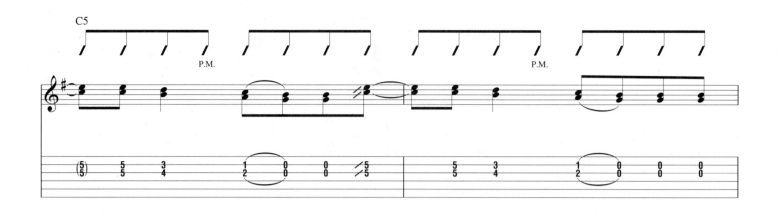

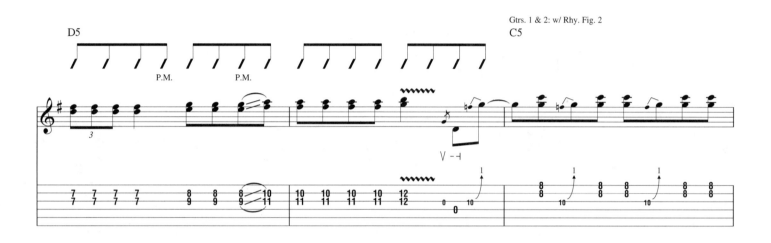

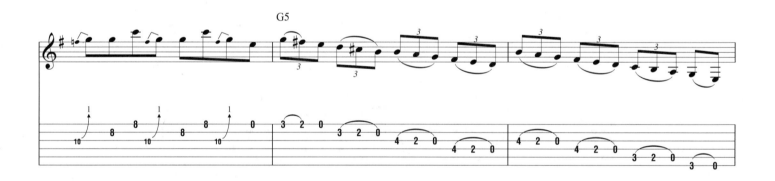

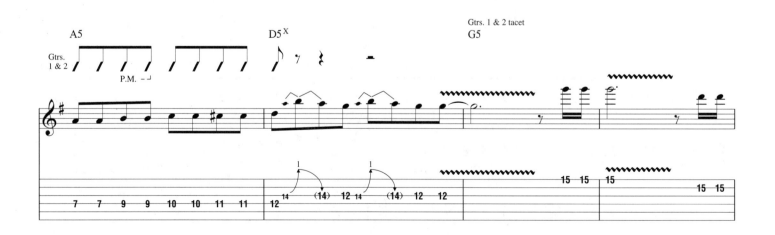

246

Chorus

Gtr. 3 tacet

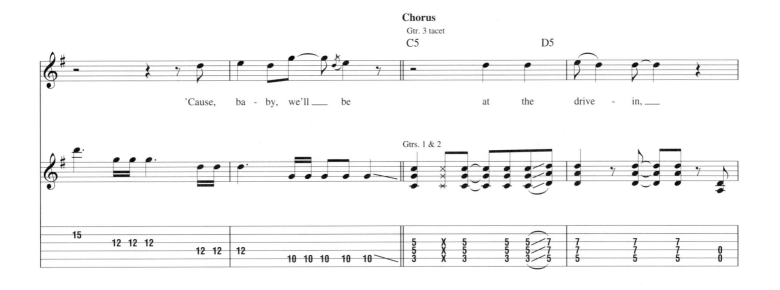

'Cause, ba - by, we'll __ be at the drive - in, __

in __ the old __ man's Ford, __ be - hind them

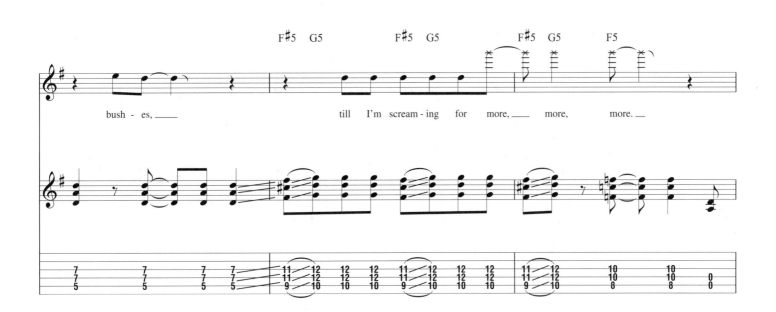

bush - es, __ till I'm scream - ing for more, __ more, __ more. __

247

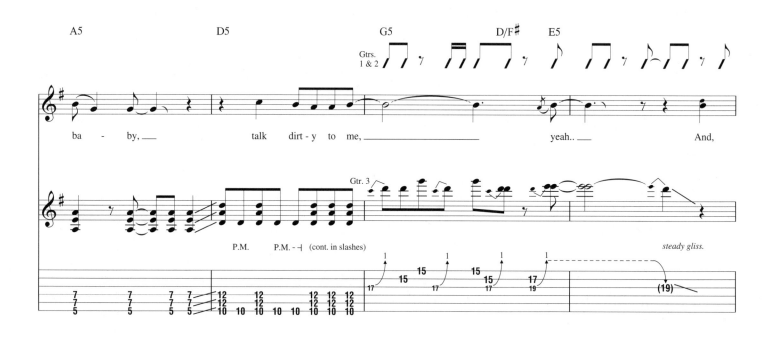

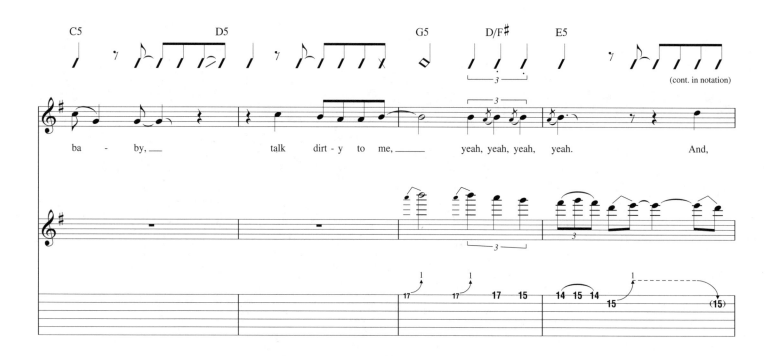

Welcome to the Jungle

Words and Music by W. Axl Rose, Slash, Izzy Stradlin', Duff McKagan and Steven Adler

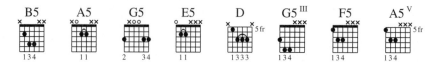

Tune down 1/2 step:
(low to high) Eb–Ab–Db–Gb–Bb–Eb

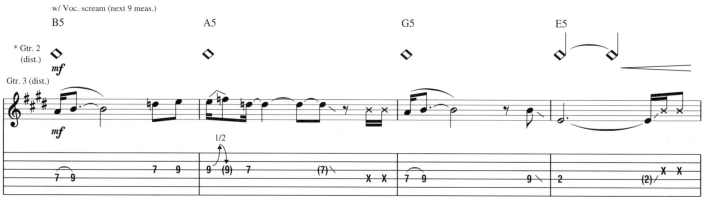

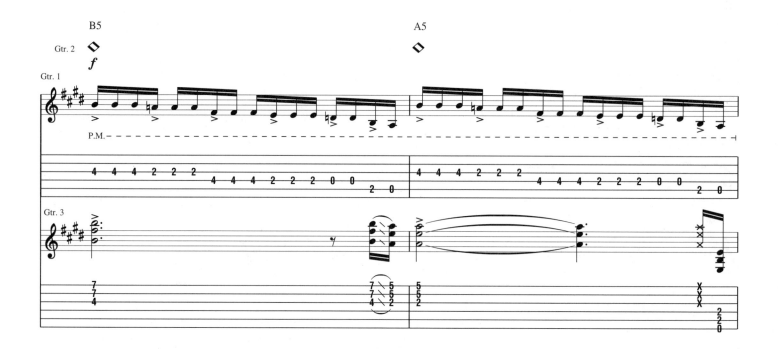

* refers to harmonic note

Verse

Gtr. 1 tacet
Gtrs. 2 & 3: w/ Rhy. Figs. 1 & 1A

| A5 | G5 | A5 | G5 F#5 E5 | A5 | G5 | A5 | G5 F#5 E5 | A5 | G5 A5 | G5 F#5 E5 |

3. Wel-come to the jun - gle, it gets worse here ev-'ry day. __ You learn to live __ like an an - i - mal, __ in the

Gtr. 1: w/ Fill 2

| A5 | G5 | A5 | G5 F#5 E5 | D5 | E5 | D5 C#5 B5 | E5 | D5 | E5 | D5 C#5 B5 |

jun - gle where we play. __ If you got a hun-ger for what you see, __ you'll take it e - ven - tu'l - ly. __

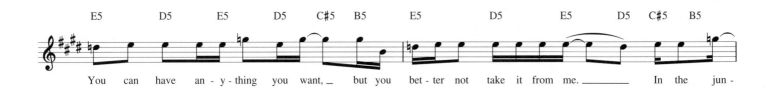

| E5 | D5 | E5 | D5 | C#5 B5 | E5 | D5 | E5 | D5 C#5 B5 |

You can have an - y - thing you want, __ but you bet - ter not take it from me. _____ In the jun -

Bkgd. Voc.: w/ Voc. Fig. 1
Gtrs. 2 & 3: w/ Rhy. Fig. 2   Gtr. 1: w/ Fill 1

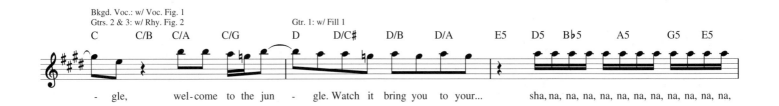

| C | C/B | C/A | C/G | D | D/C# | D/B | D/A | E5 | D5 | Bb5 | A5 | G5 | E5 |

- gle, wel-come to the jun - gle. Watch it bring you to your... sha, na, na, na, na, na, na, na, na, na, na, na,

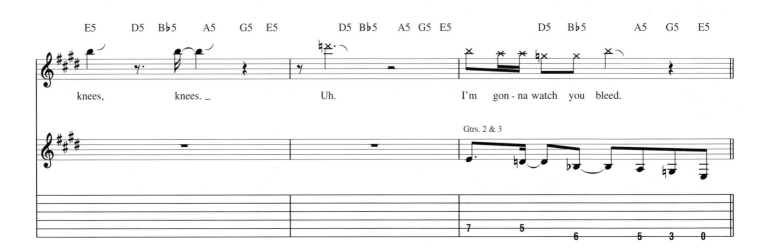

| E5 | D5 | Bb5 | A5 | G5 | E5 | D5 | Bb5 | A5 G5 | E5 | D5 | Bb5 | A5 | G5 | E5 |

knees, knees. __ Uh. I'm gon - na watch you bleed.

Gtrs. 2 & 3

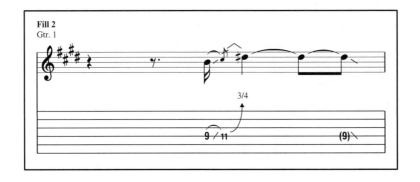

Fill 2
Gtr. 1

256

And when you're high _____ you nev - er ever want to come down,_

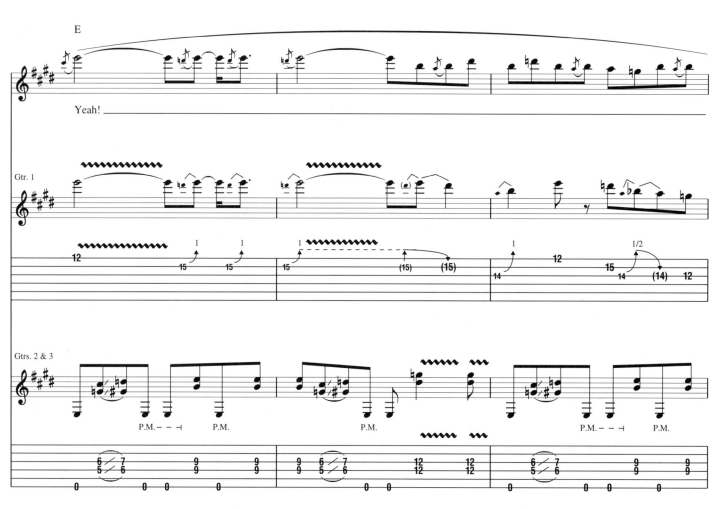

Guitar Solo

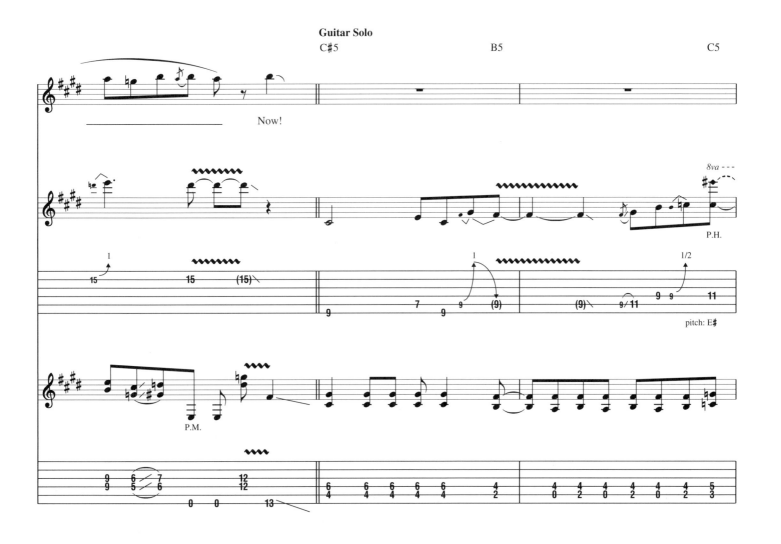

Now!

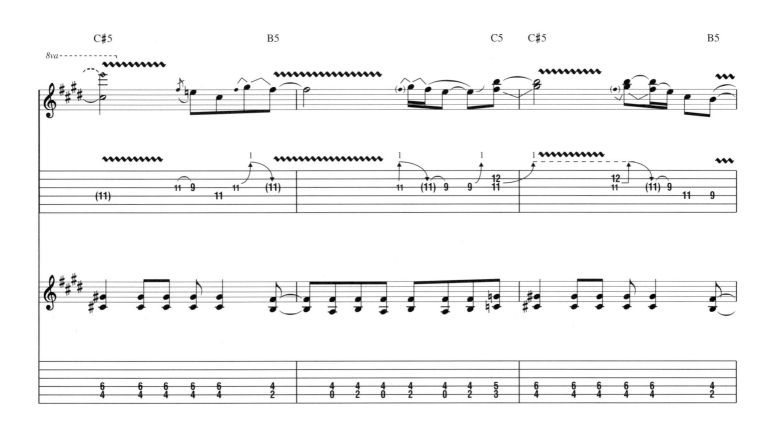

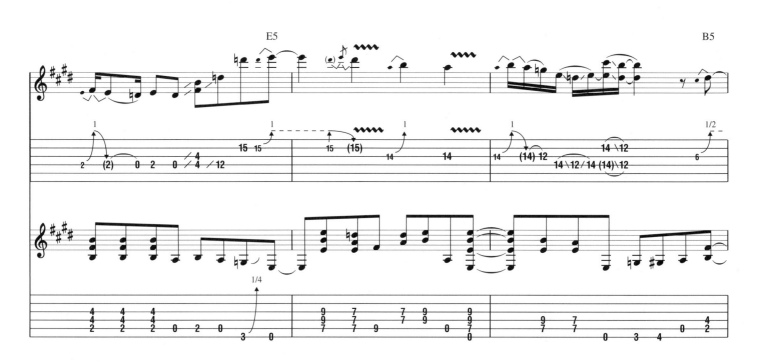

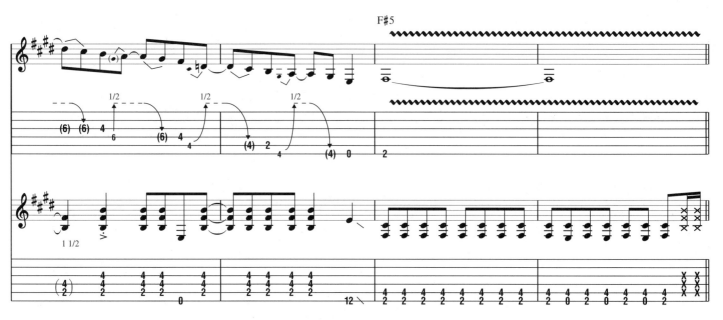

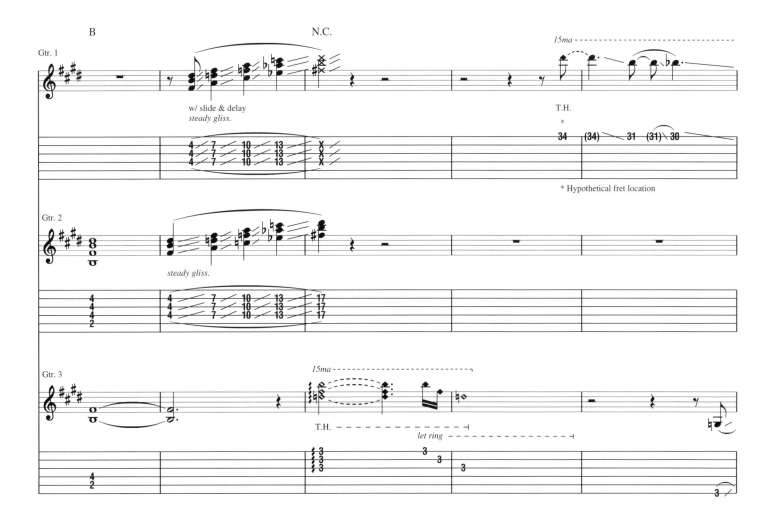

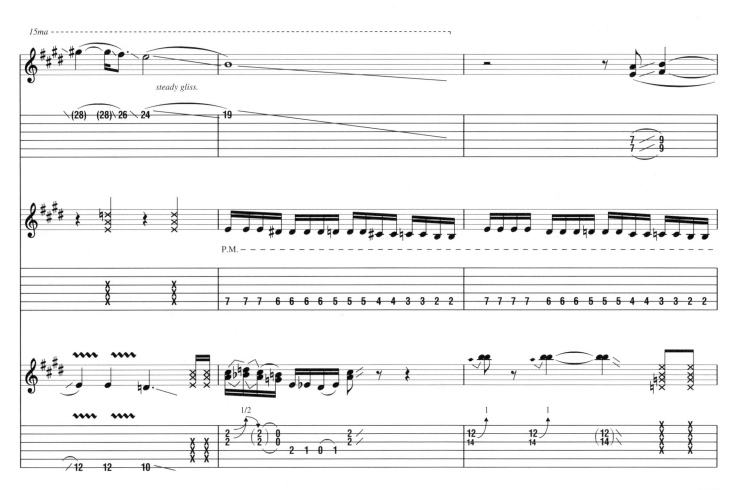

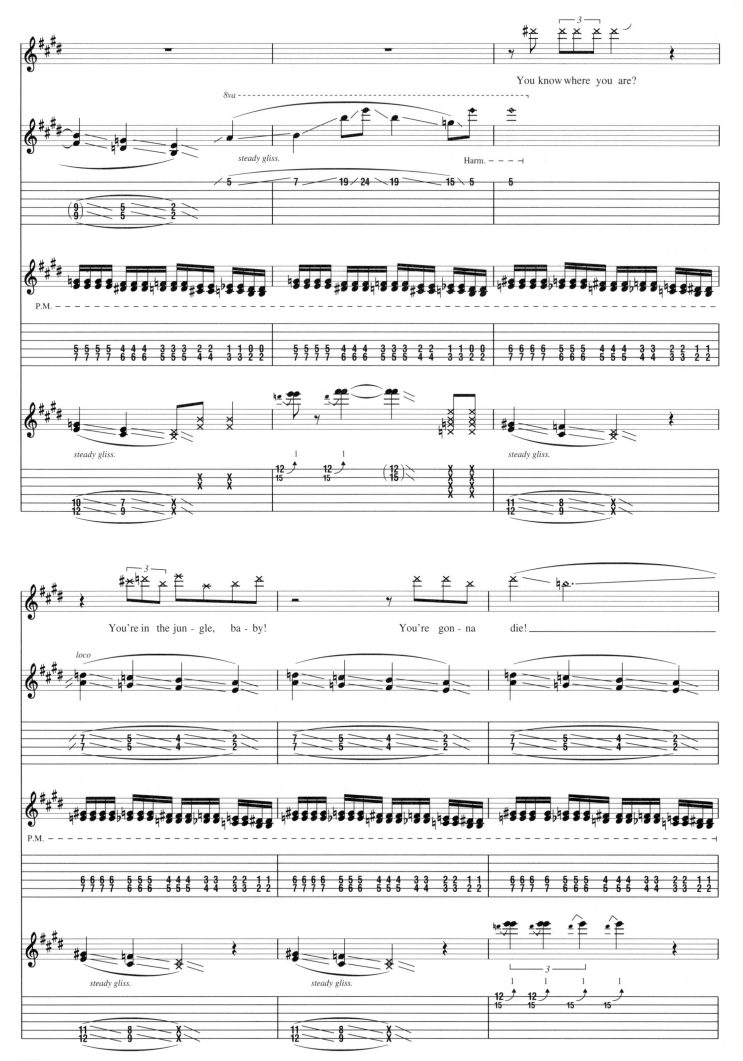

You know where you are?

You're in the jun - gle, ba - by! You're gon - na die!

When You Were Young

Words and Music by Brandon Flowers, Dave Keuning, Mark Stoermer and Ronnie Vannucci

*Chord symbols implied by bass, next 8 meas.

Interlude

Gtr. 1: w/ Rhy. Fig. 1 (2 times)
Gtr. 2: w/ Riff A (2 times)

Verse

Gtr. 1: w/ Rhy. Fig. 1 (2 times)
Gtr. 2: w/ Riff A (2 times)

Gtr. 6 tacet

4. You sit there _ in your heart - ache, wait-ing on __ some beau - ti - ful boy to,

to save you from _ your _____ old ways. _ You play for-give-ness. Watch it now, here he comes. He

Outro-Chorus

Guitar Notation Legend

Guitar music can be notated three different ways: on a *musical staff*, in *tablature*, and in *rhythm slashes*.

RHYTHM SLASHES are written above the staff. Strum chords in the rhythm indicated. Use the chord diagrams found at the top of the first page of the transcription for the appropriate chord voicings. Round noteheads indicate single notes.

THE MUSICAL STAFF shows pitches and rhythms and is divided by bar lines into measures. Pitches are named after the first seven letters of the alphabet.

TABLATURE graphically represents the guitar fingerboard. Each horizontal line represents a string, and each number represents a fret.

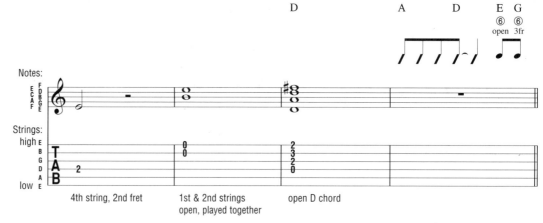

4th string, 2nd fret

1st & 2nd strings open, played together

open D chord

Definitions for Special Guitar Notation

HALF-STEP BEND: Strike the note and bend up 1/2 step.

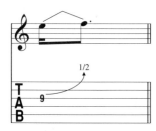

WHOLE-STEP BEND: Strike the note and bend up one step.

GRACE NOTE BEND: Strike the note and immediately bend up as indicated.

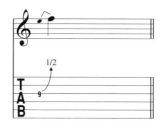

SLIGHT (MICROTONE) BEND: Strike the note and bend up 1/4 step.

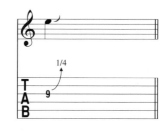

BEND AND RELEASE: Strike the note and bend up as indicated, then release back to the original note. Only the first note is struck.

PRE-BEND: Bend the note as indicated, then strike it.

PRE-BEND AND RELEASE: Bend the note as indicated. Strike it and release the bend back to the original note.

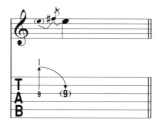

UNISON BEND: Strike the two notes simultaneously and bend the lower note up to the pitch of the higher.

VIBRATO: The string is vibrated by rapidly bending and releasing the note with the fretting hand.

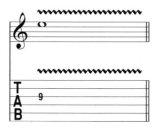

WIDE VIBRATO: The pitch is varied to a greater degree by vibrating with the fretting hand.

HAMMER-ON: Strike the first (lower) note with one finger, then sound the higher note (on the same string) with another finger by fretting it without picking.

PULL-OFF: Place both fingers on the notes to be sounded. Strike the first note and without picking, pull the finger off to sound the second (lower) note.

LEGATO SLIDE: Strike the first note and then slide the same fret-hand finger up or down to the second note. The second note is not struck.

SHIFT SLIDE: Same as legato slide, except the second note is struck.

TRILL: Very rapidly alternate between the notes indicated by continuously hammering on and pulling off.

TAPPING: Hammer ("tap") the fret indicated with the pick-hand index or middle finger and pull off to the note fretted by the fret hand.

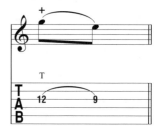

NATURAL HARMONIC: Strike the note while the fret-hand lightly touches the string directly over the fret indicated.

Harm.

PINCH HARMONIC: The note is fretted normally and a harmonic is produced by adding the edge of the thumb or the tip of the index finger of the pick hand to the normal pick attack.

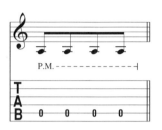

P.H.

HARP HARMONIC: The note is fretted normally and a harmonic is produced by gently resting the pick hand's index finger directly above the indicated fret (in parentheses) while the pick hand's thumb or pick assists by plucking the appropriate string.

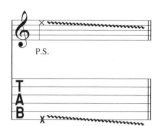

H.H.

PICK SCRAPE: The edge of the pick is rubbed down (or up) the string, producing a scratchy sound.

P.S.

MUFFLED STRINGS: A percussive sound is produced by laying the fret hand across the string(s) without depressing, and striking them with the pick hand.

PALM MUTING: The note is partially muted by the pick hand lightly touching the string(s) just before the bridge.

P.M.

RAKE: Drag the pick across the strings indicated with a single motion.

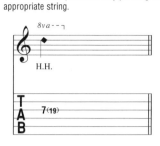

rake

TREMOLO PICKING: The note is picked as rapidly and continuously as possible.

ARPEGGIATE: Play the notes of the chord indicated by quickly rolling them from bottom to top.

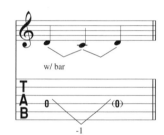

VIBRATO BAR DIVE AND RETURN: The pitch of the note or chord is dropped a specified number of steps (in rhythm), then returned to the original pitch.

w/ bar

VIBRATO BAR SCOOP: Depress the bar just before striking the note, then quickly release the bar.

w/ bar

VIBRATO BAR DIP: Strike the note and then immediately drop a specified number of steps, then release back to the original pitch.

w/ bar

Additional Musical Definitions

(accent)	• Accentuate note (play it louder).	
(accent)	• Accentuate note with great intensity.	
(staccato)	• Play the note short.	
⊓	• Downstroke	
V	• Upstroke	
D.S. al Coda	• Go back to the sign (𝄋), then play until the measure marked "*To Coda*," then skip to the section labelled "*Coda*."	
D.C. al Fine	• Go back to the beginning of the song and play until the measure marked "*Fine*" (end).	

Rhy. Fig. • Label used to recall a recurring accompaniment pattern (usually chordal).

Riff • Label used to recall composed, melodic lines (usually single notes) which recur.

Fill • Label used to identify a brief melodic figure which is to be inserted into the arrangement.

Rhy. Fill • A chordal version of a Fill.

tacet • Instrument is silent (drops out).

• Repeat measures between signs.

• When a repeated section has different endings, play the first ending only the first time and the second ending only the second time.

NOTE: Tablature numbers in parentheses mean:
1. The note is being sustained over a system (note in standard notation is tied), or
2. The note is sustained, but a new articulation (such as a hammer-on, pull-off, slide or vibrato) begins, or
3. The note is a barely audible "ghost" note (note in standard notation is also in parentheses).

RECORDED VERSIONS®
The Best Note-For-Note Transcriptions Available

ALL BOOKS INCLUDE TABLATURE

00692015 Aerosmith – Greatest Hits..................$22.95	00692931 Jimi Hendrix – Axis: Bold As Love $22.95	00694975 Queen – Greatest Hits..................$24.95
00690603 Aerosmith – O Yeah! (Ultimate Hits) $24.95	00690608 Jimi Hendrix – Blue Wild Angel.............$24.95	00690670 Queensryche – Very Best of.............$19.95
00690178 Alice in Chains – Acoustic.................$19.95	00692932 Jimi Hendrix – Electric Ladyland............$24.95	00690878 The Raconteurs – Broken Boy Soldiers $19.95
00694865 Alice in Chains – Dirt....................$19.95	00690017 Jimi Hendrix – Live at Woodstock............$24.95	00694910 Rage Against the Machine.................$19.95
00690387 Alice in Chains – Nothing Safe:	00690602 Jimi Hendrix – Smash Hits................$19.95	00690055 Red Hot Chili Peppers –
The Best of the Box..................$19.95	00690843 H.I.M. – Dark Light........................$19.95	Blood Sugar Sex Magik..................$19.95
00690812 All American Rejects – Move Along...........$19.95	00690869 Hinder – Extreme Behavior $19.95	00690584 Red Hot Chili Peppers – By the Way..........$19.95
00694932 Allman Brothers Band – Volume 1 ....$24.95	00690692 Billy Idol – Very Best of....................$19.95	00690379 Red Hot Chili Peppers – Californication $19.95
00694933 Allman Brothers Band – Volume 2 ....$24.95	00690688 Incubus – A Crow Left of the Murder $19.95	00690673 Red Hot Chili Peppers – Greatest Hits $19.95
00694934 Allman Brothers Band – Volume 3 ....$24.95	00690457 Incubus – Make Yourself.................$19.95	00690852 Red Hot Chili Peppers –
00690865 Atreyu – A Deathgrip on Yesterday $19.95	00690544 Incubus – Morningview..................$19.95	Stadium Arcadium..................$24.95
00690609 Audioslave...............................$19.95	00690790 Iron Maiden Anthology $24.95	00690511 Django Reinhardt – Definitive Collection....$19.95
00690804 Audioslave – Out of Exile.................$19.95	00690730 Alan Jackson – Guitar Collection.............$19.95	00690779 Relient K – MMHMM..................$19.95
00690884 Audioslave – Revelations.................$19.95	00690721 Jet – Get Born.........................$19.95	00690643 Relient K – Two Lefts Don't
00690820 Avenged Sevenfold – City of Evil.............$22.95	00690684 Jethro Tull – Aqualung....................$19.95	Make a Right...But Three Do $19.95
00690366 Bad Company – Original Anthology,	00690647 Jewel – Best of.........................$19.95	00690631 Rolling Stones – Guitar Anthology $24.95
Book 1..................$19.95	00690814 John5 – Songs for Sanity $19.95	00690685 David Lee Roth – Eat 'Em and Smile..........$19.95
00690503 Beach Boys – Very Best of..................$19.95	00690751 John5 – Vertigo........................$19.95	00690694 David Lee Roth – Guitar Anthology............$24.95
00690489 Beatles – 1..............................$24.95	00690845 Eric Johnson – Bloom $19.95	00690031 Santana's Greatest Hits $19.95
00694929 Beatles – 1962-1966....................$24.95	00690846 Jack Johnson and Friends – Sing-A-Longs and	00690796 Michael Schenker – Very Best of...........$19.95
00694930 Beatles – 1967-1970....................$24.95	Lullabies for the Film Curious George $19.95	00690566 Scorpions – Best of.....................$19.95
00694832 Beatles – For Acoustic Guitar...............$22.95	00690271 Robert Johnson – New Transcriptions........$24.95	00690604 Bob Seger – Guitar Collection $19.95
00690110 Beatles – White Album (Book 1) $19.95	00699131 Janis Joplin – Best of....................$19.95	00690803 Kenny Wayne Shepherd Band – Best of $19.95
00692385 Chuck Berry............................$19.95	00690427 Judas Priest – Best of....................$19.95	00690857 Shinedown – Us and Them $19.95
00690835 Billy Talent.............................$19.95	00690742 The Killers – Hot Fuss....................$19.95	00690530 Slipknot – Iowa..................$19.95
00692200 Black Sabbath –	00694903 Kiss – Best of.........................$24.95	00690733 Slipknot – Vol. 3 (The Subliminal Verses)..$19.95
We Sold Our Soul for Rock 'N' Roll...........$19.95	00690780 Korn – Greatest Hits, Volume 1 ....$22.95	00120004 Steely Dan – Best of.....................$24.95
00690674 blink-182..............................$19.95	00690834 Lamb of God – Ashes of the Wake $19.95	00694921 Steppenwolf – Best of....................$22.95
00690831 blink-182 – Greatest Hits $19.95	00690875 Lamb of God – Sacrament $19.95	00690655 Mike Stern – Best of.....................$19.95
00690491 David Bowie – Best of....................$19.95	00690823 Ray LaMontagne – Trouble $19.95	00690877 Stone Sour – Come What(ever) May $19.95
00690873 Breaking Benjamin – Phobia.............$19.95	00690679 John Lennon – Guitar Collection $19.95	00690520 Styx Guitar Collection $19.95
00690764 Breaking Benjamin – We Are Not Alone $19.95	00690781 Linkin Park – Hybrid Theory..............$22.95	00120081 Sublime..................$19.95
00690451 Jeff Buckley – Collection $24.95	00690782 Linkin Park – Meteora $22.95	00690771 SUM 41 – Chuck $19.95
00690590 Eric Clapton – Anthology................$29.95	00690783 Live – Best of.........................$19.95	00690767 Switchfoot – The Beautiful Letdown $19.95
00690415 Clapton Chronicles – Best of Eric Clapton ..$18.95	00690743 Los Lonely Boys........................$19.95	00690830 System of a Down – Hypnotize $19.95
00690074 Eric Clapton – The Cream of Clapton $24.95	00690876 Los Lonely Boys – Sacred $19.95	00690799 System of a Down – Mezmerize $19.95
00690716 Eric Clapton – Me and Mr. Johnson $19.95	00690720 Lostprophets – Start Something...............$19.95	00690531 System of a Down – Toxicity $19.95
00694869 Eric Clapton – Unplugged $22.95	00694954 Lynyrd Skynyrd – New Best of..............$19.95	00694824 James Taylor – Best of....................$16.95
00690162 The Clash – Best of.......................$19.95	00690752 Lynyrd Skynyrd – Street Survivors............$19.95	00690871 Three Days Grace – One-X $19.95
00690828 Coheed & Cambria – Good Apollo I'm Burning	00690754 Yngwie Malmsteen – Anthology...........$24.95	00690737 3 Doors Down – The Better Life $22.95
Star, IV, Vol. 1: From Fear Through the	00690754 Marilyn Manson – Lest We Forget $19.95	00690683 Robin Trower – Bridge of Sighs $19.95
Eyes of Madness $19.95	00694956 Bob Marley– Legend $19.95	00690740 Shania Twain – Guitar Collection...........$19.95
00690593 Coldplay – A Rush of Blood to the Head.....$19.95	00694945 Bob Marley– Songs of Freedom $24.95	00699191 U2 – Best of: 1980-1990................$19.95
00690838 Cream – Royal Albert Hall:	00690657 Maroon5 – Songs About Jane $19.95	00690732 U2 – Best of: 1990-2000................$19.95
London May 2-3-5-6 2005 ....$22.95	00120080 Don McLean – Songbook $19.95	00690775 U2 – How to Dismantle an Atomic Bomb ...$22.95
00690856 Creed – Greatest Hits $22.95	00694951 Megadeth – Rust in Peace $22.95	00690575 Steve Vai – Alive in an Ultra World $22.95
00690401 Creed – Human Clay $19.95	00690768 Megadeth – The System Has Failed...........$19.95	00660137 Steve Vai – Passion & Warfare $24.95
00690819 Creedence Clearwater Revival – Best of.....$19.95	00690505 John Mellencamp – Guitar Collection........$19.95	00690116 Stevie Ray Vaughan – Guitar Collection.......$24.95
00690572 Steve Cropper – Soul Man $19.95	00690646 Pat Metheny – One Quiet Night............$19.95	00660058 Stevie Ray Vaughan –
00690613 Crosby, Stills & Nash – Best of...............$19.95	00690558 Pat Metheny – Trio: 99>00 ....$19.95	Lightnin' Blues 1983-1987..................$24.95
00690289 Deep Purple – Best of....................$17.95	00690040 Steve Miller Band – Young Hearts $19.95	00694835 Stevie Ray Vaughan – The Sky Is Crying $22.95
00690784 Def Leppard – Best of $19.95	00690794 Mudvayne – Lost and Found................$19.95	00690015 Stevie Ray Vaughan – Texas Flood $19.95
00690347 The Doors – Anthology....................$22.95	00690611 Nirvana $22.95	00690772 Velvet Revolver – Contraband $22.95
00690348 The Doors – Essential Guitar Collection $16.95	00694883 Nirvana – Nevermind $19.95	00690071 Weezer (The Blue Album)................$19.95
00690810 Fall Out Boy – From Under the Cork Tree ..$19.95	00690026 Nirvana – Unplugged in New York $19.95	00694447 The Who – Best of.....................$24.95
00690664 Fleetwood Mac – Best of..................$19.95	00690807 The Offspring – Greatest Hits $19.95	00690589 ZZ Top Guitar Anthology.................$22.95
00690870 Flyleaf $19.95	00694847 Ozzy Osbourne – Best of $22.95	
00690808 Foo Fighters – In Your Honor $19.95	00690399 Ozzy Osbourne – Ozzman Cometh $19.95	
00690805 Robben Ford – Best of....................$19.95	00690866 Panic! At the Disco –	
00694920 Free – Best of...........................$19.95	A Fever You Can't Sweat Out $19.95	
00690848 Godsmack – IV $19.95	00694855 Pearl Jam – Ten $19.95	
00690601 Good Charlotte –	00690439 A Perfect Circle – Mer De Noms.............$19.95	
The Young and the Hopeless $19.95	00690661 A Perfect Circle – Thirteenth Step...........$19.95	
00690697 Jim Hall – Best of........................$19.95	00690499 Tom Petty – Definitive Guitar Collection $19.95	
00690840 Ben Harper – Both Sides of the Gun $19.95	00690826 Pink Floyd – Dark Side of the Moon..........$19.95	
00694798 George Harrison – Anthology..............$19.95	00690789 Poison – Best of.......................$19.95	
00692930 Jimi Hendrix – Are You Experienced?.........$24.95	00693864 The Police – Best of.....................$19.95